THE SILENT STRUGGLE

D1513314

The Complete Guide to Taking Charge of **ADHD in Adults**, New Powerful Strategies to Master Your Moods, Embrace Neurodiversity, Accept Yourself, and Thrive, for Today's Men and Women

L.William Ross-Child M.L.C

Nova Mundo Press, an indent of Nova Mundo Publishing Ltd

137b Westlink House 981 Great West Road

Brentford TW8 9DN United Kingdom

"Overcome the notion that you must be regular. It robs you of the chance to be extraordinary." – Uta Hagen

Copyright

Copyright © 2022 by Nova Mundo Publishing Ltd & L. William Ross-Child

All rights reserved.

No portion of this book may be reproduced in any form without written permission from the publisher or author, except as permitted by U.S. copyright law.

For information:

novamundopublishing@gmail.com

ISBN: 978-1-80361-462-5

Cover Art by NM Design

Interior Design by Nova Mundo

COPYRIGHT PROTECTION WARNING

The author has registered this work at ProtectMyWork.com

© Copyright 2022 Nova Mundo Publishing Ltd
All Rights Reserved.
Protected with Protect My Work.com
Reference Number: 17145280322S009

Table of Contents

Introduction 1

ADHD Facts 2

Diagnosis in Adults..11

ADHD in Men vs. Women...18

The ADHD Differently Wired Brain 32

ADHD and Sexuality 37

Acceptance Is the Key 39

Anger Management for Men and Women 45

Emotional Regulation 49

Impulsivity...65

The Perfectionism Shame and the Frustration Wheel 77

Find Your Strengths and Weaknesses 87

ADHD and Relationships...94

ADHD in the Workplace...98

ADHD in the Family 101

Fitness and Outdoor Sport......................................109

Alternative Therapies 114

Conclusion 124

References 128

A GIFT for YOU

Thanks a lot for choosing my book. I have 4 complementary books that I think you will love. You can download your gift by scanning the QR code on page 126.

☑ **1.MINDSET** Motivate Yourself for Success by Karen Hopkins

☑ **2.INVESTING IN YOU** The Power of Positive Thinking by Tony J. Adams

☑ **3. STOP PROCRASTINATING** The Power of NOW by Tony J. Adams

☑ **4. ADHD MEDICATIONS & FOOD** What you need to know by L.William Ross-Child

☑ **5. ADHD Coloring Book** by Nova Mundo

Or write to: novamundopublishing@gmail.com "ADULTS"

You can listen to the audio version of this book for FREE while you read along. Please scan below or click the link: rb.gy/dfzcgf

Introduction

The silent struggle is what most adults with ADHD are going through. This is even more true for the many who did not get a diagnosis and don't have a name for their daily feelings of inadequacy. A patient of mine expressed how he felt for many years before getting a diagnosis. When he could finally give a name to how he felt and why he had always felt that way, he said, "I felt like I was trying hard to fit a square peg into a round hole most of the time in my life."

I imagine you can relate to such a definition. I know the struggle you have been through firsthand because ADHD has always been my companion. Giving a name to your feeling of discomfort can produce a kind of relief.

Perhaps you thought, 'Am I lazy, stupid, or just crazy?' Did you feel different from others? Sometimes, did you wonder why you reacted in a certain way or could not be like everybody else? I'm sure you will love the chapter about the "differently wired brain." When I discovered the information in this chapter, it was revealing, to say the least. Imagine that you are the only red-haired person in your country.

Would you think, 'What's wrong with me?' Probably everyone else would support the idea that something was wrong with you. Now imagine that one day you discovered that it was just a question of a *"genetic variant that causes the body's skin cells and Ghair cells to produce more of one particular type of melanin and less of another"* (Healthline.com). So, it's just a question of more or less melanin. It has nothing to do with you being strange, inferior, or wrong. It's a simple genetic variation, like blue or green eyes.

I know you get the point! Similarly, ADHD has a genetic cause. Dopamine plays a big role. We all go through a silent struggle due to the lack of studies and research on the topic. ADHD is probably the most misunderstood, mistreated, and undervalued syndrome of our time. In an adult diagnosis, the same method used to assess the syndrome's incidence for children 30-40 years ago is still used today. For example, sexuality is not even mentioned. Despite many significant findings, there are still controversial opinions on ADHD. I think it is time for people with ADHD to gain the knowledge that opens up a completely new and positive outlook for a brighter and happier future.

After all, Leonardo da Vinci, Albert Einstein, Stanley Jordan, Eleanor Roosevelt, and Steve Jobs made history, and ADHD did not stop them from becoming great achievers. Many famous people in different fields achieved outstanding results despite, or thanks to, ADHD. This book is written with the mission to give you the key to opening up the great potential inside every one of us and shining. Turn what seemed to be a curse into a gift.

"If I cannot do great things, I can do small things in a great way." – Martin Luther King

ADHD Facts

What Is Adult Attention Deficit Hyperactivity Disorder (ADHD)?

Many people are familiar with ADHD. Some get diagnosed and, consequently, start to learn about it. Others just read about or know somebody affected by ADHD. The majority still don't have correct information about this syndrome's real nature and complexities.

You may recall children who have difficulty paying attention and children who are energetic or impulsive. Well, it is not only children who can have ADHD. It is estimated that four to five percent of adults in the United States have it; however, they are seldom diagnosed or treated.

Who Is at Risk for Adult ADHD?

Every person with ADHD is commonly diagnosed using the same parameters used for children. This is a serious failing on the part of the scientific community. Given the ever-increasing number of adult men and women with ADHD, this should be remedied as soon as possible. Some people may be diagnosed early and are aware of their condition.

On the other hand, some are not diagnosed early and find out about it only later. While many children with ADHD receive support, approximately 60 percent of adults struggle with the condition. Adult Attention Deficit Hyperactivity Disorder (ADHD) appears equally prevalent in both sexes. There is currently no one-size-fits-all treatment for ADHD. If a person's doctor determines that they have it, the person and doctor will work together to develop a treatment plan specific to the person's needs.

A combination of sustained difficulties, such as trouble paying attention, impulsive conduct, and hyperactivity, is characterized by ADHD. Adult ADHD may result in unstable relationships, poor job performance, very low self-esteem, and many other issues.

Though it is referred to as adult ADHD, indications begin in early infancy and last throughout maturity. ADHD is often not noticed or diagnosed until adulthood. The symptoms of this disorder in adults may be less evident than they are in children, but they are still present. Adults may experience a decrease in impulsivity, but they may also continue to struggle with hyperactivity, restlessness, and difficulty paying attention.

Treatment for adult ADHD is quite like the treatment for pediatric ADHD. The treatment for adult ADHD involves medication, psychological counseling, psychotherapy, and treatment for many other co-occurring mental health disorders such as bipolar disorder.

If a person has adult ADHD, they may find it challenging to do the following:

- Comply with instructions.

- Keep information in mind.

- Concentrate.

- Plan for tasks.

- Complete jobs on time.

These symptoms can range in severity from mild to severe, and their severity can change over time. They can cause issues in a variety of settings, including the family and the workplace. Receiving ADHD therapy and learning how to manage the condition is highly beneficial. Most adults with ADHD learn to adapt to their surroundings. They may also discover their unique talents and achieve success.

Is ADHD a Disability?

Learning can be a test for anyone. It could be challenging if you have a few issues that influence your conduct, consideration, and concentration. It should be noted that ADHD is not classified as a learning disability. However, research suggests that 30 to 50 percent of people with ADHD may also have specific learning disabilities that combine to produce a more challenging learning environment. Because of how ADHD people's brains function, they need a visual learning experience to perform. Unfortunately, this world of teaching and learning is based on a linear, data-driven system. In chapter 4, we will go in-depth into this topic. According to the National Institute of Mental Health, ADHD is more noticeable in certain children in early elementary school than in preschool. More than two million children in the United States alone have attention deficit hyperactivity disorder (ADHD), implying that at least one child in a typical study hall of 24 to 30 children could have ADHD. ADHD is not a learning disability, but it can be determined to be one under the Individuals with Disabilities Education Act (IDEA), making a student eligible for special education services.

Dispelling Myths About ADHD

There are a lot of misconceptions about ADHD. As an adult with ADHD, you may hear a variety of misinterpretations that make it difficult to know what to believe and what is the best help offered.

However, as previously stated, the ability to comprehend comes with information, and understanding the facts allows you to be more confident in making informed decisions. Here are some common myths about ADHD:

ADHD Is Not a Real Medical Condition

According to the National Institute of Health, the Centers for Disease Control and Prevention, and the American Psychiatric Association, ADHD is a medical condition. You should not believe anyone who tells you differently, especially someone who isn't an expert. ADHD is a genetic disorder, and one out of every four people with it has a parent who also has it. According to imaging studies, there are differences in mental health between children with and without ADHD. Furthermore, neuroimaging studies have shown that ADHD children have neurodivergent brains compared to neurotypical children.

Bad Parenting Causes ADHD

Again, this myth should be dispelled from people's minds. People with ADHD will struggle with specific behaviors. If you are a parent of a child with ADHD, some people who don't know you or your child may attribute their behavior to a lack of discipline. They don't realize that inappropriate remarks or constant squirming are symptoms of a disorder, not poor parenting.

Individuals with ADHD Need to at Least Try to Pay Attention

People with ADHD require the same things as those who do not have ADHD – love, kinship, understanding, focus, and appreciation from their loved ones. They make a good effort, but we must recognize that it is difficult for them to focus. It isn't for lack of motivation. Simply telling people to concentrate is akin to telling a farsighted person to not wear glasses. According to scientific evidence, there are differences in the pathways or neural organizations in the cerebrums of people with ADHD. These organizations take longer to create or work less productively than in people who do not have ADHD.

People with ADHD Cannot Focus

People who are easily agitated find it challenging to shift their attention away from activities they enjoy. A child who is reading their favorite space book, for example, may be hyper-focused on what they are doing. Keep in mind that while people with ADHD can be intensely focused, they may not be focusing in the same way as someone who does not have ADHD.

All Individuals With ADHD Are Hyperactive

Hyperactivity or impulsivity is not a symptom that all people with ADHD experience. There are three types of ADHD. The most common is ADHD combined, the least common is impulsive/hyperactive, and the inattentive and distractible type is characterized by inattention and distractibility without hyperactivity. This type, also known as attention deficit disorder (ADD), does not affect activity levels.

Only Boys Have ADHD

While it is true that young men are more likely to have ADHD than young women, this does not mean that only boys experience ADHD. Young men have more pronounced symptoms and side effects. On the other hand, young women have more clearly defined signs and manifestations. The symptoms in young women may go unnoticed. According to research, young men and young women have different levels of mindfulness. Young women with ADHD frequently have less difficulty focusing and exhibit less impulsivity than do young men with ADHD. They will, however, appear to be more daydreamy and distracted.

Girls With ADHD Do Not Experience Hyperactivity

While young women with ADHD are less hyperactive than young men with ADHD, this does not mean they don't experience hyperactivity at all. Hyperactivity just looks different in girls than it does in boys. To young women, hyperactivity may come in the form of being extremely touchy or overly passionate. They may disrupt discussions or even be more chatty than other girls. While this does not appear to be an indication of ADHD, it very well could be a side effect. As a result, many young women are misdiagnosed because their symptoms are not as obvious as those of boys.

Medication Is the Only ADHD Treatment Available

Treatment for ADHD will be explored further in subsequent parts; however, due to the many side effects, medication isn't the primary method of treating ADHD. Therapies and lifestyle changes can go a long way toward treating ADHD. The best option is to combine therapy, lifestyle changes, and recommended medications from your doctor. All cases are different, and treatment can depend on the severity of your case.

ADHD Is a Learning Difference

To put it simply, ADHD is not a learning disability, but it has an impact on a person's overall ability to learn. It would be difficult for children to learn because of their difficulties with concentration. A learning inability makes it difficult to master explicit concepts such as math or reading. ADHD can result in learning disabilities, which is why this misinterpretation arises. However, the fact that ADHD is not a learning disability does not mean that children should not receive academic assistance. In the following sections, we will look at the facilities and provide advice for children with ADHD. For people with ADHD, focus (hyperfocus) can be triggered by a person's interest in the task or topic of study. If there is no interest, there is no focus, and it is difficult to learn and maintain concentration.

Kids Will Outgrow ADHD When They Become Adults

While ADHD symptoms may diminish or even disappear as children grow older, this is not guaranteed. Symptoms may change as the child grows older and more complexities come their way. Individuals with ADHD will continue to have symptoms for the rest of their lives. This is why early treatment is critical for empowering them to figure out how to manage their symptoms.

What Difficulties Do ADHD Individuals Face?

Simple daily activities such as picking up the kids from game practices or finishing a project on time may be very difficult for people with attention deficit hyperactivity disorder (ADHD). Chronic hyperactivity, difficulty concentrating, not keeping track of time, procrastination, and interrupting others are some of the ways in which this disorder can contribute to derailment in everyday life. The only good news is that, with minimal forethought and a few easy changes, you may begin to overcome the difficulties presented by this disorder right now.

Getting Adequate Sleep Is a Difficult Task

According to the National Sleep Foundation, many people with attention deficit disorder have difficulty sleeping. It is hard for them to react to the internal signals indicating that it is time to calm down and prepare themselves for bed. According to Dr. Wetzel, adults with ADHD are more likely to be night owls. A planned evening routine is essential to getting decent sleep.

Keeping Up with Paperwork Is a Challenge

Is your work desk covered by a mountain of paperwork, with vital documents getting lost among the jumbled piles? Managing paperwork seems tedious but deciding whether to save something or discard it requires a degree of attention that any adult with ADHD may be unable to muster.

Being on Time for Appointments Is a Challenge

Regular punctuality is a challenge for people with attention deficit disorder, whether it involves picking up children after a playdate, getting to a doctor's appointment, or getting to work on time. You may have trouble managing time— five minutes might seem like ten, and vice versa — or you might waste time performing mundane activities like searching your wardrobe for clothing.

Objects Are Often Misplaced, Which Is a Challenge

Do you have trouble finding your keys, mobile phone, or any other accessory when you need them? Adults with this disorder are prone to misplacing or completely losing such things.

Noise Is a Constant Source of Distraction.

To people who do not have ADHD, the presence of background noise may go unnoticed. However, noise like radio or television broadcasts at home, or anywhere else, including at work, or even conversations at a restaurant, may be very distracting to those with ADHD, as they cannot shut it out.

Keeping Yourself Safe on the Road Is a Challenge

According to research, people with attention deficit hyperactivity disorder (ADHD) face much greater risks of traffic accidents and infractions than any other typical adult.

Maintaining Conversations Is Difficult

You tend to complete other people's sentences as if you already know exactly what the other person is going to say next, don't you? Having meaningful discussions with people who have ADHD and who, therefore, are always impatient may be challenging.

Keeping Track of Tasks While on the Job Is a Challenge

You've misplaced a paper indicating when you'll meet with your boss, and you can't recall whether the meeting begins at 9 a.m. or 10 a.m. When you get home from work, you have no idea if it's your turn to pick up the kids from soccer practice today. Does this sound familiar?

Prioritizing Your Day Is a Difficult Task

Knowing what you need to do first may be difficult when your planner is overflowing, and you're dealing with adult attention deficit disorder. This can make for a very stressful start to the day.

Completing Tasks Is a Difficult Task

Having adult ADHD makes it difficult to complete tasks, especially when you are concentrating on a small number of assignments at once. "People [who have] ADHD begin activities and other projects with a great deal of energy and enthusiasm, but as soon as the project progresses, that energy and enthusiasm may wane," Wetzel says.

Types of ADHD

ADHD is characterized by hyperactivity, impulsivity, and inattention. Most people who don't have ADHD also experience a certain degree of impulsive or inattentive behavior, but people with ADHD experience severe hyperactivity-impulsiveness and inattentiveness. There are three types of ADHD, each of which is linked to one or more characteristics. They are as follows:

- Predominantly Inattentive ADHD: People suffering from this type of ADHD mostly have symptoms of inattention. Their impulsive nature or hyperactivity is not as pronounced as their inattentiveness. Although at times they might struggle with hyperactivity or impulse control, these are not the main characteristics of predominantly inattentive ADHD. This type of ADHD is more common in girls than in boys.

- Predominantly Hyperactive-Impulsive ADHD: People with predominantly hyperactive-impulsive ADHD have more impulsivity and hyperactivity symptoms than they do inattention. Patients with predominantly hyperactive-impulsive ADHD may also be inattentive at times, but that is certainly not the main characteristic of this disorder. Children suffering from this disorder can cause a lot of disturbance in their classrooms. They make learning far more difficult for other students as well as themselves.

- Combination ADHD: If a person has combination ADHD, their symptoms don't fall perfectly under hyperactive-impulsive behavior or inattention. Instead, they experience a combination of symptoms of both categories.

Diagnosis in Adults

Symptoms in Adults

When ADHD is diagnosed and treated during childhood, it becomes easier to manage later in life. However, the symptoms are sometimes unnoticed, and ADHD goes undiagnosed. If it does not receive proper treatment at an early stage, it will have a greater impact in later years. To ensure appropriate management of the condition, distinguishing the symptoms, and seeking assistance from a specialist are required. In this section, I will introduce you to some of the common symptoms of ADHD in adults.

Difficulty in Focusing

An inability to focus is an indication of ADHD. This difficulty can escalate to the point where an individual misses out on a significant opportunity because they are unable to concentrate due to their condition. In this book, you will learn a few techniques to help increase your focus.

Hyperfocus

In the past section, we discussed the challenges individuals face regarding focus. However, the opposite effect is also common in adults with ADHD. It is known as hyperfocus. As you might guess from the name, hyperfocus is a state in which the individual is so engrossed in the task at hand that they cannot look away. They concentrate with great intensity on that single task, and their behavior differs significantly from that of distractibility. Often, individuals have no idea how many hours have passed while they have been hyper-focused on a single task.

Problems with Managing Time

This is yet another characteristic of adults who have ADHD. Often, adults with ADHD can't figure out how to effectively invest their energy and complete all the tasks on their daily agendas. People with ADHD are frequently seen as sluggish or passing up opportunities. Some people even forget about invitations to gatherings and weddings. Individuals with ADHD have a very different response to time and a different view of the time required to complete a specific assignment. Some analysts and specialists have coined the term "time visual impairment," which refers to the problem of managing time. Furthermore, the fact that ADHD makes them easily distracted exacerbates the situation when it comes to time management.

Disorganization

Adults with ADHD often fall behind on their monthly payments, or their workspace is always in shambles. In the worst cases, people lose their jobs or careers because of their disordered behavior. They are constantly fatigued and overwhelmed by the growing weight of work that is left unfinished. Nonetheless, if proper procedures are followed, these side effects can be avoided. Because of ADHD, each person's needs are unique. As a result, one must carefully consider which techniques to use.

Impulsiveness

Impulsivity is also a common symptom of ADHD in adults. This means that adults with ADHD make decisions without fully considering them. This specific side effect can manifest in a variety of ways. Furthermore, not everyone with ADHD experiences it. Some common ways in which these characteristic manifests are completing tasks in a hurry, saying things that are considered inappropriate in friendly settings, intruding on a discussion out of nowhere, and getting things done without considering the gravity of the outcomes that are to follow. A close examination of a person's shopping habits may best determine whether they are impulsive.

Forget Things Easily

People are perplexed by this side effect because we all forget things from time to time. Does this mean that we all have ADHD? No. However, people with ADHD may often exhibit symptoms of forgetfulness. They are constantly looking for normal things like keys or glasses because they keep losing them. They may even miss clinical appointments or fail to respond to messages. The main issue here is whether ADHD causes the neglect. It has a negative impact on people's lives and harms relationships. When ADHD adults have significant responsibilities, such as caring for a child, the neglect becomes unsettling. There have been instances in which a parent failed to pick up their child from school or dance lessons due to their condition.

Hypercritical

Adults with ADHD are remarkably self-aware, and they are harsh on themselves. The main reason for this is that they are so concerned about not finishing work on time or dealing with personal setbacks that their confidence suffers. They begin to judge themselves severely for even the most negligible errors. They don't see things clearly, and everything is portrayed negatively. As a result, everything from indiscretion to difficulty focusing contributes to being hypercritical.

Mood Swings

We all experience eagerness, nervousness, and a wide range of emotions, which can manifest as mood swings. However, in people with ADHD, these emotions are amplified. These emotional outbursts influence their jobs and personal lives as well. People with ADHD may feel as if they have no control over the situation. Managing ADHD symptoms in everyday life can be seen as a difficult task, and if these issues are not addressed, they may accumulate and cause a more significant problem in the future. It is essential to recognize that you have a great deal of control over managing your ADHD. Don't let the outside world tell you who you are or what you have to offer. You may notice that your confidence and moods improve as you learn to advocate for yourself.

Absence of Motivation

Adults with ADHD frequently don't feel spurred to do things like others do. The foundation of this problem lies in how these individuals can't concentrate; subsequently, they feel unmotivated to finish the tasks with responsibility. Furthermore, as you are aware, being overpowered is extremely common in ADHD adults, which adds to the feeling of being unmotivated. Many people do not attempt to complete a task and instead give up far too soon. They are unable to determine the proper path between various points. They can't focus on one thing at a time and keep bouncing around from one errand to the next. As a result, nothing is ever finished.

Fatigue

People frequently overlook the fact that one of the primary symptoms of ADHD is fatigue. I understand that this revelation may astound you. However, there is a simple explanation for this. People who have ADHD are frequently hyperactive, which causes them to feel tired. People with ADHD are also subjected to the adverse effects of opposing sleeping patterns.

Furthermore, in some people, fatigue is caused by the constant battle that they must engage in to focus on their daily tasks. Another explanation is that the medications prescribed for ADHD cause people to feel exhausted all of the time. Whatever the cause, the primary concern is that fatigue is hard to handle and can make life difficult.

Anxiety

Many people believe that they must constantly move and that there is no moment of harmony in life. This is the reason why people with ADHD are so anxious. Another reason people with ADHD become anxious is that they can't remember important details. Furthermore, people trying to deal with sleep issues can also experience more difficult situations leading to anxiety.

All of the ADHD side effects in adults mentioned in this section can result in several personal and professional issues. These difficulties, however, are manageable. In the following sections of this book, you will learn how to manage them. If you want to know why ADHD occurs, the section that follows will provide plenty of information.

ADHD Diagnosis

ADHD is one of the most common neurodevelopmental syndromes in adults. It is frequently discovered in children because of disruptions in the classroom. Inattention (an inability to focus), hyperactivity (moving around excessively or inappropriately for the surroundings), and impulsivity (acting without thinking) are easy to spot. On the other hand, symptoms could be regarded as attitude or character flaws in adults.

Many patients with ADHD have noticed an increase in disturbing symptoms during COVID-19. Although online self-assessment tools can help you determine whether you have ADHD-like symptoms, you will need to arrange an in-person session to complete diagnosis and treatment. Meanwhile, read about what to expect during screening and how to get started if you are diagnosed with ADHD.

Examinations by Professionals

At the end of your session, your healthcare professional will inform you whether you have ADHD or any other health conditions. Following that, they will go over treatment options with you and, if necessary, recommend specialists for more screening and care.

An in-depth interview and physical exam by a healthcare specialist can confirm an ADHD diagnosis. Diagnostic criteria, however, differ slightly depending on whether the patient is an adult or a youngster.

Suppose you are looking for an ADHD evaluation and you are an adult. In that case, you must contact a licensed mental health worker such as a clinical psychologist, neurologist, psychiatrist, primary care physician, or social worker.

To determine whether you have ADHD, they will conduct a thorough assessment based on the diagnostic criteria outlined in the American Psychological Association's Diagnostic and Statistical Manual of Mental Disorders (DSM-5). That's the national standard for the appropriate diagnosis and treatment of mental health conditions in the United States.

According to the DSM-5 Criteria for ADHD, children up to the age of 16 must exhibit at least six symptoms of inattention and hyperactivity-impulsivity. However, only five signs are required to diagnose ADHD in adults and adolescents aged 17 years or older. Symptoms may appear differently in older ages; for example, adult hyperactivity can manifest as extreme restlessness.

Labs and Examinations

An interview and physical exam are the gold-standard diagnostic procedures to uncover ADHD symptoms and any potential mental and physical health issues.

Although you may have heard of many ADHD tests, the syndrome cannot currently be diagnosed exclusively through brain imaging examinations such as an MRI, PET, or CT scan. However, your doctor may advise you to undergo blood tests, brain imaging examinations, or an electroencephalogram (EEG) to rule out other health issues.

Self-Assessment/At-Home Testing

While there are many online self-assessments and questionnaires for ADHD symptoms, the majority are not scientifically tested or standardized. As a result, you should not use them to self-diagnose or to diagnose others. Again, you must see a qualified and licensed healthcare provider to receive a correct diagnosis.

However, if you are unsure whether your symptoms are truly those of ADHD, you can use the World Health Organization's (WHO) Adult Self-Report Scale (ASRS) Screener to identify the signs and symptoms of ADHD in adults.

If you are concerned that your beloved may have ADHD, the first step is to consult with a healthcare specialist to see if the symptoms match the diagnosis. A mental health expert, such as a psychologist, psychiatrist, or primary care physician (e.g., a pediatrician) can make the diagnosis.

How Is ADHD Identified?

To diagnose ADHD, healthcare providers follow the American Psychiatric Association's Diagnostic and Statistical Manual, Fifth Edition (DSM-5) recommendations. This standard diagnostic aids in ensuring that patients with ADHD are properly diagnosed and treated. Using the same criteria across areas also assists with identifying how many adults have ADHD and how this disease affects public health.

Here are the criteria in a nutshell. Please bear in mind that they are given for your convenience. ADHD can be diagnosed and treated only by experienced healthcare professionals.

ADHD in Men vs. Women

ADHD in Men

The distraction, disorganization, and impulsive personality characteristics of ADHD affect all areas of a patient's life. But for men, attention deficit hyperactivity disorder brings double challenges, especially in their professions and relationships. A study from 2015 revealed that ADHD diagnoses more than doubled from 1999 to 2010. Another study said that ADHD medicine usage has increased, though the use of medicine by children has somehow decreased.

The scientific evidence in ADHD is often related to men because hyperactivity in men is much more noticeable. The general symptoms of ADHD are difficulty staying focused and paying attention, uncontrollable behavior, and hyperactive performance. Being a developmental disorder, ADHD continues into adulthood in more than 80 percent of childhood cases.

Symptoms of ADHD in Adult Men

ADHD in men is much more visible, but it might be hard to distinguish it and admit it, even for the person himself. The reason is that, today, most men do not pay attention to their bodies through pains and aches. When you add in all the ADHD challenges related to executive functions, most of these men also end up acquiring physical problems.

So, before any of these physical problems start showing up, it is essential to recognize and treat ADHD. To do so, look for the following symptoms.

Impulsive Behavior

Men take more time to come back from conflicts than most women do. With ADHD, men might feel more agitated with constant criticism and remarks made about their performance, outlook, or presentation of ideas.

This leads them to lie, isolate, and become expressively distant from others. They might also engage in voluntary activities like drinking, overeating, or overspending.

Emotional Instability

It is hard for men with ADHD to express themselves in front of others. Society grooms boys from a young age to be hard and tough, and they feel emotionally stranded once they grow up. Expressing themselves in front of others takes a lot of strength and courage, whether it's a professional association or emotional bonding.

Impossible to Pay Attention

They often zone out during meetings, conversations, and arguments. It might look like they do not care or do not want to be a part of it. However, the fact is, they can't concentrate on anything for long.

Feeling Demotivated All the Time

ADHD in a man reduces motivation and makes it hard for him to finish anything he started. It is not laziness but a sign that he has no enthusiasm to finish something.

Engagement in Unnecessary Arguments With Others

The fluctuating moods and emotional distress often let him engage in unnecessary disputes or verbal fights with others.

Increased Chances of Missing Important Deadlines or Events

Men with ADHD are also more likely to forget important events, miss deadlines, or be late for necessary appointments. They do not do it on purpose; it is just something they cannot control.

Sensitive to Criticism

Many individuals reported feeling more sensitive to receiving criticism for their actions. Fear of rejection, mockery, taunts, and disapproval indicates rejection-sensitive dysphoria (RSD), which can be present in ADHD-affected people.

Disapproval from Others

An intense emotional response is shattering for people with ADHD. It is hard for them to accept any withdrawal or criticism. They are not emotionally fragile, but disapproval from others is much more intense for them than it is for neurotypical people.

Expressing Stress or Pain

If emotional pain persists, a person with ADHD also experiences sadness, discomfort, and stress, which affects his self-esteem.

ADHD in Men Can Be More Noticeable

ADHD affects both men and women in similar ways. However, in men, it is much more noticeable. The symptoms of ADHD can change a man's professional and personal life in the following ways.

At Work

Men with ADHD often find it hard to get along with other people. They look agitated but often give up on any situation easily. They do not find most things exciting and are more likely to fail all job roles assigned. Compared to women, men are more likely to express themselves through their job and profession. However, this differential behavior is the biggest hurdle they face when it comes to their career.

They often feel stressed and pressured, and even regular work feels like a burden. All these manifestations of ADHD limit their capability and progress in their career. Ultimately, the pressure affects their work quality. Either they quit their job or they are laid off or fired.

At Home

People with attention deficit hyperactivity disorder (ADHD) experience more emotional collapses than people without ADHD. People often characterize such people as "too sensitive," but it's more than a mood swing. ADHD has neurological associations that cause uncontrollable emotional episodes.

A man with ADHD typically faces more severe episodes of any emotion, but it might affect his relations if he shows more aggression or anger. People around him may step back so that they do not have to deal with his emotional instability. The inability to express himself makes an ADHD patient a loner. It also increases his risk of suffering stress-related disorders, i.e., anxiety and depression.

The societal expectation of a man to be stronger, dominant, and emotionally stable sometimes supports such outbursts of anger and emotion. Many people do not even realize that they have a medical issue that needs treatment. Instead, they justify their rage by putting down other people or blaming them for the situation.

Recovering from Conflict

Men find it more difficult to resolve a conflict than women do. Men become more agitated and disturbed when a problem arises, resulting in more aggression. They are also more sensitive to criticism than women are, which jeopardizes their performance at home and work. This implies that men are more likely to seek distractions to avoid conflict than women are. Most of the time, men are emotionally distant, untruthful, or assertive. Women, on the other hand, are better at conflict resolution.

Emotions All Bottled Up

For more than 80 percent of men, expressing their feelings while having ADHD symptoms is extremely difficult. Society and culture raise men in a way such that everyone expects them to be "manlier" by being more emotionally stable and sturdy. However, this is not possible every time. So, when a man with ADHD is in such a situation, he hides his true feelings instead of expressing himself. This lack of emotions results in more problems in both one's personal and professional life, putting men in immediate need of professional help.

Denial

Men, in general, are less responsive to the idea of having ADHD than women are. It is too hard for them to process this information, and this denial leads to self-criticism, making their condition worse. Sometimes they reject this label, fearing the blame that might fall on them for failing in their careers or relationships. In addition, they sometimes blame their uncontrollable actions on their partners and friends, as this seems easier than risking the diagnosis of ADHD.

ADHD in Women

Attention deficit disorder (ADHD or ADD) is not a gender-inclined disease. Contrary to the popular belief that ADHD affects only men, its symptoms can also show up in women; however, they are often undiagnosed. The diagnostic tools and approaches for ADHD are the same for men and women, but the signs vary.

The difference in symptoms is the primary reason why it is difficult to determine whether a woman has ADHD. There is already so much happening inside a woman's body, i.e., hormonal shifts, that sometimes they describe ADHD symptoms as "just another bad day." Only a doctor can diagnose a correct statement, but there are noticeable changes that might represent a medical condition even before one goes to the doctor.

Early Signs of ADHD in Young Girls

The signs of ADHD in women start to appear at an early age. Depending on the severity and frequency of these symptoms, they might not become evident until puberty. However, this is not a universal truth, and many women are left undiagnosed all their lives.

The common ADHD symptoms in a young girl are as follows:

- Difficulty in concentration

- Disobedience

- Forgetfulness

- Aggressive attitude

- Loud and clumsy personality

- Frequent fidgeting

Attention deficit disorder in adult women shows up more persistently, but it is less evident than it is in men. A study reports that most women do not consider getting a checkup for ADHD unless any of their kids are diagnosed. Considering that ADHD has a genetic linkage, mothers and their kids often get a diagnosis together.

As opposed to situation with ADHD in men, ADHD-positive women are quieter and show inattentive behavior. They also find it hard to simultaneously manage work and personal tasks, irrespective of their nature. They become unhappy and dissatisfied with themselves because of this, and stress and anxiety often add to typical ADHD symptoms. This added stress is why the ADHD symptoms in women differ from those in men. Some of these symptoms include the following.

Distraction

Most women with ADHD are easily distracted and, therefore, are unable to perform well. Additionally, they do not stand out and are often ignored or forgotten. Due to this behavior, they often become targets for neglect and carelessness by their loved ones and family. A significant number of women never get diagnosed because they do not show hyperactivity or any other noticeable sign even if they experience this symptom.

Failure to Multitask

Organizational skills and executive functions are a big challenge for women with ADHD. Managing time often feels challenging, and a multi-step task is next to impossible for them. They are more likely to miss a deadline or lose important papers while multitasking. According to a 2014 review study, women with ADHD are more likely to exhibit subjective symptoms that are not observable. However, even if they lack managerial skills, women can develop better work plans than men. As a result, teachers, parents, and sometimes pediatricians miss these ADHD symptoms in young girls.

Underachievers

In the case of ADHD, most women do not prominently show ADHD symptoms until they start college. Currently, these women often show poor management skills or no self-regulation, which are the earliest signs of ADHD. However, the behavioral changes of such women are not as apparent as hyperactivity in men. This is why only one-third of women showing inattentiveness seek medical help during this time. Later, the symptoms are even more visible when they enter practical life. This delay in symptoms is why women are generally diagnosed in their middle ages and not in childhood.

Mood Swings

Short temperament and mood disorders are a lot more common in women with ADHD. Because of this, these women are unable to think clearly, which affects their relations and social life.

Mood swings are not a significant sign of ADHD, so mood disorders and other symptoms can lead to a better diagnosis.

Low Self-Image

Women with ADHD also exhibit low self-esteem; they experience weight problems, stress, anxiety, and eating disorders more than otherwise healthy women. These situations can arise at any stage of life and are not confined to adulthood.

Unreliable

As with men, society grooms women to follow specific gender-based standards. Everyone expects a girl to be a better planner, organizer, conflict manager, and a more reliable person. For women with ADHD, filling all these roles is difficult, as they are unable to think and act like the average person.

Ignoring the Symptoms

Changing perspectives on anything and fluctuating thoughts are not unique to an ADHD patient; they are also related to several other diseases. However, this inconsistent thinking is distressing for ADHD patients, dragging them to drastic polarities. They could either be motivated or lazy, highly organized or very messy, creative, or dull-minded. Most importantly, they ignore all these symptoms, considering them "normal. " It's their brain that picks a side, and it's not the same side all the time. This changing tendency prohibits their growth and learning, causing them to keep everything inside.

More Inattentive

Though not familiar to all, many medical experts believe that women generally show inattentive behavior. According to psychiatrists, nine general symptoms are associated with an inattentive presentation of ADHD in women.

- Trouble focusing on work, home tasks, or games

- Inability to pay attention to details and making careless mistakes

- Feeling difficulty in all organization-related duties and activities

- Finding distractions in everything

- Failing to comply with instructions

- Forgetting ordinary things such as paying bills

- Avoiding everything that involves focusing such as filling out forms

- Losing things whenever they are needed

- Being absentminded during direct conversations or meetings

Additional Challenges for Women With ADHD

If a girl with ADHD does not receive a diagnosis until adulthood, she often suffers through many other conditions as well. For example, stress, depression, and anxiety are the three biggest challenges for anyone who is suffering from ADHD. With low self-esteem and self-confidence, managing stress is even more complicated. All these factors collectively cause work and relationship problems for young women. They might also lead to underachievement in different aspects of their lives.

The Health Risks of Undiagnosed ADHD in Women

If untreated, ADHD can negatively affect women's health. First, it is rare for a woman with ADHD to manage her problems. Second, even if she does, she is under constant stress, which could lead to many diseases such as high blood pressure, digestive problems, chronic pain, and heart problems, all of which will have long-term effects on her health.

On the other hand, getting a timely diagnosis would make it easier for them to cope with the symptoms. Instead of considering ADHD as normal emotional behavior, it is necessary to recognize it as an abnormality.

Why Girls and Women Are Under-Diagnosed

Boys are more likely than females to be diagnosed with ADHD for a variety of reasons. Below are some important factors:

- Women and girls with ADHD tend to internalize rather than externalize their feelings.

- Women and girls with ADHD are less hyperactive and more inattentive.

- Women and girls with ADHD may have comorbid psychiatric disorders like depression and anxiety.

- Women and girls with ADHD may have comorbid obsessive-compulsive disorder, frequently accompanied by perfectionist behaviors that can mask symptoms and delay diagnosis.

- Women and girls with ADHD are usually not referred well by others, and treatment requires a referral.

- Covert aggression is more prevalent in women and girls with ADHD than overt aggression.

- Women and girls with ADHD have a lower proclivity for physical aggression than boys.

ADHD manifests itself in various ways in different individuals. The main symptoms may be influenced by sex, gender, and hormones.

Gender stereotypes may prevent instructors from identifying signs of ADHD in female students. Because symptoms in females may be milder, doctors may be hesitant to identify them as ADHD if the patients also exhibit signs of emotional problems.

Because, until recently, most research has focused on males, more is understood about how guys have ADHD and its effects on their lives.

Gender norms may drive females to conceal and disguise ADHD symptoms. Stereotypes about neatness, organization, collaboration, compliance, and social behavior may lead girls and women in schools and family systems to ignore or adjust to their ADHD symptoms.

Hormonal Fluctuations

Hormonal changes that begin in adolescence continue to significantly impact the lives of females with ADHD. Their monthly hormonal changes aggravate the difficulties they face because of their ADHD. Several women say that the anxiety of being the main parent of kids with ADHD while also struggling with their ADHD approaches emergency levels every month during their menstrual period, which may last up to a week. Although the proportion of older women with ADHD has yet to be determined, it is fair to assume that hormonal changes linked with menopause would increase ADHD signs of emotional reactivity.

Low estrogen levels have been linked to decreased cognitive performance, particularly poor auditory recall and word retrieval, and PMS. These intellectual deficits and the impaired executive performance observed in ADHD can serve as a trigger for referring older females who were formerly able to operate at a high level and who now face the low estrogen condition linked to early menopause.

Instead of Having a Support System, They Become a Support System

Women are often cast in the position of caregivers, both at work and at home. While males with ADHD are usually encouraged to surround themselves with a support system, few women have such access. In fact, society has historically expected women to provide the support system.

The rise of "dual-career couples" has exacerbated the difficulties faced by women with ADHD. During most of the last two decades, an increasing number of women have been expected to perform the more conventional duties of mother and wife, working effectively and relentlessly while juggling the responsibilities of a full-time job.

Boobs, Periods, and ADHD in Girls

Girls with ADHD have an uphill fight from the start. Because the symptoms of ADHD in girls are different from those in males, ADHD in girls is more likely to go undiagnosed or misdiagnosed.

Evidently, boobs, menstrual periods, and eyeliner aren't enough to hurl at a middle-schooler; symptoms in females generally emerge around the beginning of puberty.

In women, ADHD frequently manifests as symptoms of inattention rather than hyperactivity. As a result, inattention is frequently dismissed as a character flaw rather than a condition.

School Daze

When females with ADHD enter college and are no longer surrounded by the rigidity of their parents, curfews, and obligatory school attendance, things start to become interesting. Women with ADHD, for example, are known to live in the fast lane while having a nervous breakdown on the inside over the ever-growing mound of schoolwork they haven't even begun to complete.

Taking Care of Their Children While Neglecting Themselves

A female with ADHD should concentrate on therapy for herself when she wants to be the perfect mom for her kid, much as normal flight instructions urge parents to put on their personal oxygen masks before helping their children.

Helping children with ADHD operate better involves their parents' full involvement in understanding and regularly using excellent parenting methods, establishing home schedules, and educating the kid to see their ADHD as a positive, productive problem-solving tool. Consequently, when it comes to assisting her kid, the best approach for a mother with ADHD is to get herself treated for and educated about ADHD.

Manic Pixie Nightmare

According to research, women with ADHD have an unpleasant propensity to keep their issues (and dishes) to themselves, keeping no one in the loop about the turmoil and worry that is steadily taking over their lives. This may be because they never got a proper diagnosis and, thus, did not have recourse to beneficial medicines and coping techniques. When you are completely aware of the fact that you have ADHD, it is very easy to get consumed by feelings of guilt when you have fallen behind in your obligations.

Regrettably, the society in which we live still places more expectations on women in certain areas. Did you forget to send your friend a birthday card this year? Were you distracted when a buddy wanted you to pay close attention to something? If so, you might consider yourself to have failed.

Diagnosing ADHD in Women

Most people believe that ADHD is a disease that affects hyperactive schoolboys. Women are frequently not diagnosed until maturity, as the way ADHD presents in females does not match this stereotype. If you suspect that you have ADHD but haven't been formally diagnosed, make this your top priority. When you've been diagnosed, you will feel better about yourself. Knowing the cause and the reason for your inner feeling is the first step to thriving.

According to one study, after being diagnosed with ADHD, women seemed able to accept their previous errors and feel more in command of their present circumstances. They were relieved to know that they weren't insane and that there was a term for what they had been going through.

Hyperactivity in Women

Women may be classified with hyperactivity-impulsivity ADHD, but it is less common than inattentive ADHD in women. Hyperactivity comes with its own set of difficulties. You may discover that you have more vitality than your classmates and that you are always chatting. You may recall being rejected, criticized, and ostracized by your classmates because you seemed to be different. This can be carried into maturity.

Symptom Presentation

Women are more likely than males to internalize their symptoms. Girls' symptoms are more focused on inattentiveness and disarray. Families and peers are less likely to be cognizant of these symptoms for diagnosis, as such symptoms are frequently overlooked.

Comorbid Psychiatric Disorders

Because females' ADHD symptoms are less disruptive, mood disorders are often identified before the possibility of ADHD is explored. ADHD seldom travels alone. Therefore, you may be suffering from one or more additional comorbidities. Try not to be frightened. Knowing what additional conditions you have, if any, enables you to address them individually, allowing you to live the healthiest life.

Signs of one disease may sometimes be confused with symptoms of ADHD and vice versa. Most people with ADHD have at least one comorbid syndrome, which may include personality disorders.

Personality Disorders

It's critical to tell your doctor about all of your symptoms and concerns. Being open about your feelings does not mean that you are whining. Your doctor wants to understand how you're feeling and what you're going through so that they can provide you with the best treatment possible.

Coping Strategies

Women may be able to conceal the negative consequences of their ADHD symptoms if they acquire stronger coping mechanisms than their male counterparts. Many people, for example, overcompensate by creating lists to keep themselves organized. While this method is effective, it makes it extremely easy for physicians to overlook the diagnosis.

Women's ADHD symptoms may worsen as they get older. For example, when the educational framework is no longer productive and the standard is higher, ADHD symptoms may begin to cause more struggles.

Tips for Women With ADHD

When women learn that they have ADHD, they often feel relieved. They may have hated themselves for their failures for years, and their consciousness has suffered as a result. Emotional, mental, and bodily fatigue may have resulted from their constant concern with every aspect of their lives.

They have an answer now. They have been diagnosed with ADHD, and they recognize that their illnesses are not their fault. Feelings of inadequacy may go away once individuals understand that they have ADHD, putting them in a good situation to effectively manage their symptoms.

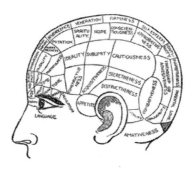

The ADHD Differently Wired Brain

Understanding how the brain of a person with ADHD is wired is the foundation for dealing with ADHD. The brain controls our actions, such as speaking, reacting, learning, and perceiving the reality around us. We can represent the ADHD brain's way of thinking as a big circle.

It represents how an ADHD brain functions. An ADHD brain – or, better, an ADHD mind – works in a circular way instead of a linear way. What does that mean? It means a lot! But before we dig into it, we must understand that there are two types of brains: the neurotypical brain and the neurodivergent or neurodifferent brain.

ADHD people have neurodivergent brains and, consequently, a neurodivergent mind. The neurodivergent mind had a different way of seeing, learning, and feeling than the neurotypical mind. Now let's go back to the big circle image for a second; it represents how a neurodivergent mind functions.. It functions in a circular way but lives in a linear world.

Let's consider an example. In college, we learn by using the linear method. We learn by reading and memorizing data. Generally speaking, we study notions in a sequence. I'm not saying that this method is wrong or doesn't lead to results. What I'm saying is that with ADHD, it's challenging to learn anything in this way. We are more visual, intuitive learners and the data-driven system is dull and unattractive to us.

ADHD people have a hard time performing or learning anything that is not catching their interest. Neurotypical people can easily learn things that are boring or not interesting to them if this is required to reach an objective. Neurodivergent brains have a hard time doing so. Scientific evidence shows why this is so; we will go through the scientific part later in this chapter. An example can help you better understand how it all functions. Imagine you have two computers: a Mac and a PC. From the outside, they look the same. Inside, they are wired differently, which means if you press the same commands on the keyboard, you will have different functions due to the different wiring systems.

That's the way neurodivergent and neurotypical differ one from the other. Facing the same situation, you will have two distinct responses because the brains are wired differently.

There's not a right way or a wrong way of being in this case. Each has its purpose and utility. For many years, or since always, the circular minds of ADHD-affected people were considered an inferior way of being, thinking, and generally speaking, indicating a lower intellectual capacity. Being labeled as "lazy, chaotic, uncontrollable, stupid, disturbing other people's work, and probably never succeeding in anything" was familiar for ADHD-affected people. Being divergent in our society was never a gift but mainly a curse.

By now, slowly, something else is emerging. Even if the majority of people don't understand, a new feeling is making its way to the top. The neurodivergent could be just the resource we all need. Studies were conducted to measure the capability for problem-solving by comparing neurotypical and neurodivergent young students.

Four groups were formed, each made up of five people. Two groups were exclusively neurotypical, while two groups contained three neurotypical and two neurodivergent ADHD students. Note that the ADHD students were diagnosed but had never taken medication for the condition, which means no pills.

The problem to be solved was the same, and the students were in the same college class and at the same level.

The first two groups started to solve the problem in a classical linear way: data-driven, research, and analysis. The other two groups, including the ADHD students, had another experience. The ADHD students made jokes and engaged in considerations that were not congruent with the problem to be solved. In these two groups, the discussion was informal, and the impression, from the outside, was that they lost focus on the problem. But suddenly, the groups with ADHD people were able to find unexpected, creative, unusual solutions. The visual, imaginative approach made them faster and better than the groups with only neurotypical students.

Does this mean that neurodivergent is better? No! But it shows the capacity of the circular, visual way of the mind to be of great help in this world. In fact, some of the most outstanding geniuses who improved the way we live were ADHD-affected. People like Leonardo da Vinci, Albert Einstein, and Thomas Edison had ADHD.

They deserved it, and recognition of their achievements will help us remember the great potential we receive as a gift. Still, we need to understand and develop that potential to make it shine. That's where this book comes in handy: to help you understand, find solutions, and have a thriving life.

Major companies have already realized the potential of the ADHD mind. They saw that integrating circular and linear minds into their teams leads to better results. The neurodivergent are usually intuitive and creative, but they lack organization skills, which are qualities of neurotypical, linear minds.

The combination of the two is the best you can have.

Scientific Evidence

You may be surprised to learn that ADHD is, in fact, one of the underlying problems associated with decreased dopamine levels (a significant synapse). ADHD was also one of the primary emotional wellness issues that responded strongly to the prescriptions used to treat dopamine deficiency. When adults or children with ADHD are examined, it is discovered that their dopamine levels are deficient.

The synapse movement is seriously impacted in four central areas of the cerebrum in ADHD patients. These useful regions are as follows:

- Frontal Cortex – The frontal cortex region maintains responsibility for everything from executing to organizing to maintaining concentration. Inattention is often caused by a reduction in dopamine levels in this part of the brain. The executive functions are also affected, as is the ability to organize.

- Basal Ganglia – Next, we come to the brain region that is responsible mainly for maintaining proper communication between different parts. The basal ganglia can be called a neural circuit in simple terms. Whenever a part of the brain has to relay information to another part, it first comes to the basal ganglia. It is then sent to that part of the brain where it needs to be communicated. When the basal ganglia do not have adequate dopamine levels, she undergoes a "short circuit" phase, which causes impulsiveness and attention loss.

- Limbic System – Unlike the other parts, the limbic system is situated in the depths of the human brain, and its primary function is the manifestation of emotions. When dopamine is deficient in this region, emotions are no longer stable, and the person suffers from restlessness and loss of attention.

- Reticular Activating System – Your brain has more than one pathway. One of the most critical relay systems is the reticular activating system. If this system faces any deficiency in dopamine levels, the instant result is hyperactivity, impulsivity, and inattention.

Likewise, you must remember that legitimate working of the mind is possible when these areas of the cerebrum interface with each other to work in a synchronized manner. A dopamine deficiency prevents that from happening. So, if even one of these four regions, or all four regions, has a problem with dopamine, ADHD might occur.

There is no substantial confirmation regarding what part of the cerebrum is liable for ADHD side effects. More clinical preliminaries and experience are needed to say anything explicitly. The nature of ADHD treatment will work better when the comprehension of these neurochemicals increases.

Neuroimaging

Neuroimaging has been a source of great hope lately due to the capability of tracing brain connections more precisely than ever. Whether the results are trustworthy is still a matter of contention among scientists. However, neuroimaging has resulted in a giant step forward in tracking brain activities. I'm sure that decisive discoveries will be made in the near future.

"Everybody is a genius. But if you judge a fish by its ability to climb a tree, it will live its whole life believing that it is stupid." **Albert Einstein**

ADHD and Sexuality

ADHD's impact on sexuality may be difficult to quantify. That's because each person's sexual symptoms may vary. Certain sexual symptoms may cause sexual dysfunction. This may put a lot of strain on a relationship. Understanding how ADHD impacts sexuality may help a couple deal with stress in their relationship. Sadness, emotional immaturity, and anxiety are all typical symptoms of ADHD.

All of these factors may have an adverse effect on sexual desire. Maintaining order and structure, for example, may be tiring for someone with ADHD. They may not have the enthusiasm or energy to participate in sexual activities.

Certain sexual symptoms may cause sexual dysfunction. That may put a lot of strain on a relationship. Understanding how ADHD impacts sexuality may help a couple deal with stress in their relationship.

Women with ADHD can have a hard time achieving orgasm. Some women claim to be able to have multiple orgasms in a short period, while others claim to be unable to achieve orgasm despite extended stimulation.

Hypersensitivity is a possibility in people with ADHD. This implies that a sexual activity pleasurable to a partner who does not have ADHD may be annoying or uncomfortable to a person with ADHD. To someone with ADHD, the smells that often precede intercourse may be unpleasant or irritating. Also, for someone with ADHD, hyperactivity is a barrier to intimacy. A companion with ADHD may find it difficult to relax sufficiently to be in the best mood. Most ADHD cases appear to be the result of a different brain development that begins before birth. That can result in an atypical brain structure, improper message transmission, and low chemical activity within the brain.

Hypersexuality and hyposexuality are two sexual symptoms associated with ADHD. If an individual with ADHD has sexual problems, they may fit into one of these groups. It's also worth noting that sexual symptoms aren't included in the American Psychiatric Association's accepted diagnostic criteria for ADHD.

Hyposexuality and ADHD

An individual's sex drive plummets, and they frequently lose interest in sexual activities, which is the opposite of hypersexuality. This may be a result of the ADHD itself. It may also be a secondary effect of medicine, especially antidepressants, often given to individuals with ADHD and other attention deficit hyperactivity disorders.

For someone with ADHD, sexual activity is no different from any other activity that presents difficulty. They may have trouble focusing during sex, lose interest in what they're doing, or get distracted.

Hypersexuality and ADHD

If you are hypersexual, you have an abnormally strong desire for sex. Sexual arousal produces endorphins and activates neurotransmitters in the brain. That can create a sense of serenity, which helps to alleviate the restlessness that is frequently associated with ADHD. Promiscuity and pornographic usage, on the other hand, may cause relationship problems. It's essential to remember that promiscuity or the use of pornography isn't part of the ADHD diagnosis criteria.

Due to impulsive issues, some individuals with ADHD can engage in hazardous sexual behavior. Also, people with ADHD are more likely to develop drug abuse problems and have impaired decision-making abilities, leading to sexual risk-taking.

Acceptance Is the Key

Once you realize that you have ADHD, you can do certain things to make your life easier.

Acknowledge Your Condition

Knowing that you have ADHD motivates you to look for ways to manage it. You can better accept and embrace your diversity by learning more about your condition and finding solutions to it. Unfortunately, many people initially hide their diagnoses. That's a mistake, as denial will only make matters worse.

While a diagnosis does present certain complexities in your life, it doesn't need to ruin it. You can live a wonderfully happy and productive life, but only if you are willing to acknowledge your condition and seek help. Accept your situation and find your strengths in the many positive benefits of ADHD. Many of the qualities that accompany this condition can be seen as superpowers. Accepting and embracing your condition and everything it has to offer can help you live a more fulfilling life.

Manage Distractions

Observe what distracts you and remove it from your environment. Display a "do not disturb" or "silence please" sign in your workplace. You can listen to white noise through earphones to help yourself focus. Some people find it difficult to concentrate when the television is on or when other distractions are present. If this is not the case, determine what is interfering with your productivity and work to eliminate it.

Take Care of Yourself

Having ADHD can make you forget to do routine activities to maintain your health. Set a schedule for washing clothes, getting your nails trimmed, seeing the dentist, and other things necessary to keep yourself healthy and groomed. Not only will this protect your health but it will also help you live a well-adjusted life.

Exercise

Exercise can stimulate the brain and improve your focus. Also, exercise releases chemicals and endorphins that increase your overall well-being. It's not about simply losing weight and being attractive. Training is about becoming a healthier person in mind and body. To start, get your body moving for at least 15 to 30 minutes every other day.

Get Enough Sleep

Lack of sleep drains brainpower and has terrible effects on physical health. However, a good night's rest replenishes your energy and makes you think clearly. So, be merciful to yourself and sleep for as long as you need to.

Reduce Stress Levels

Stress hampers your ability to overcome your ADHD traits. Find time to relax and unburden yourself. Avoid stressors as much as possible. Break overwhelming tasks into simpler ones. Do not dwell on negative emotions. They will only make it worse.

Enhance Your Self-Control

Self-control is dependent on your stress level, so you need to find ways to reduce it. It is also affected by your ability to be calm. You can attain a state of calmness through the following methods:

- Take at least 10 deep breaths: Emotions weaken self-control and are affected by breathing. The slower you live, the calmer you get.

- Clear your mind: Thoughts fuel temptations and wild emotions. Affect the way you feel by silencing your mind. Please don't force it, though, because it might frustrate you even more. Simply observe what's going on in your head without supporting it. The thoughts lose their energy after a while and gradually fade.

- Imagine a relaxing scene: Recall the moments when you are at peace or imagine a scenario in which you are completely calm and unaffected. Being in control also involves knowing what is truly important for you and acknowledging your behaviors' consequences.

- Think about your priorities: What are you living for? What are the essentials in your life? What will you protect, and what will you discard in favor of your priorities? Be serious about this. Doing this can change the way you live your life.

- Think about the pros and cons of doing anything: Stop if you know that acting upon an impulse is not 100 percent beneficial to you. Just stop right there and pull out a piece of paper and a pen. List the pros and cons of going through with your impulse. Do not make excuses so that you can indulge in that behavior. Imagine the negative consequences and honestly evaluate whether they are worth suffering to achieve a little fun.

- Keep your priority list and your pros and cons list where you can easily access them. You get easily distracted by what's in front of you, right? Don't allow yourself to get sidetracked. Keep your lists in a location where you can see them before you do anything that you might regret later.

You can amplify self-control by exercising your willpower regularly. Practice simple things such as finishing an easy task every day or writing more legibly. Reward yourself whenever you achieve something out of self-discipline. That will train your mind to anticipate rewards every time you take on a challenge that requires willpower.

Self-control can mean diverting your attention toward things that matter. Know your weaknesses and plan how to avoid them before you encounter them. That way, the decision to refuse temptation will become automatic.

Instead, stimulate your mind with more meaningful and rewarding activities.

Use Lists

Lists help bring structure to a mind that flies off in all directions. Write lists. They are valuable because:

- Writing makes you pay attention.

- Keeping a record ensures that you have something to refer to if you forget what you've written.

- You can compare the result of a task to what you intended to do.

- It helps you organize your thoughts and activities.

Use Planners

Planners assist you in creating schedules and managing your time in accordance with your priorities. It's nice to be able to cross things off a list every now and then. If it works for you, this method may be useful. In your planner, make a list of your doctors' appointments, work obligations, and social obligations so you can check on them when an important occasion comes up.

Keep a Journal

Having ADHD means that a lot of things are going on in your mind. Keep a journal so that you can write down whatever is bugging you. That will free your mind of bothersome thoughts and create opportunities for problem-solving. Journal writing is also a safe way to process emotions.

Set Timers and Alarms

Your sense of time is not as sharp as that of people without ADHD. Use timers and alarms to remind you of deadlines. Countdown timers are particularly helpful in creating a sense of urgency that will motivate you to work on a task. Also, timers and self-imposed deadlines will keep you from spending too much time on something that engrosses you. Finally, timers can help you begin a task and stick with it. Set the timer for 15 minutes and, during that time, do not work on anything except that single task. Take a break for five minutes. You may find that you are willing to continue for another 15 minutes.

Tidy Up

Although it may be hard for you to clean up your clutter, it will significantly help increase your overall productivity. A mess can distract you, even though you might say that you don't mind working in a cluttered environment. When your space is organized, you will quickly find the things you need.

Practice Saying No

Your abundance of energy and narrow perspective may cause you to take on more responsibilities than you can handle. Help yourself by limiting your obligations. It will help to list what you need to do to determine whether you can complete everything on time. Then, when somebody tries to add to the list, say no. Delegate responsibilities to others if you can.

Aim for Consistency

Manage the confusion that ADHD causes by keeping things as predictable as possible. Establish routines and designate places where you'll keep your things.

Develop Helpful Skills

Gain valuable skills such as willpower development, conflict management, etc. You can learn on your own through self-help books and online material, or you can join classes. Some classes are geared toward people who have ADHD.

Get Support

Living with ADHD is a challenging experience that you don't have to go through alone. Reach out and find people to help you cope with your condition. Family and friends will likely understand because they have known you for a long time.

In addition, counselors, psychologists, coaches, and other pros have the expertise to give you expert assistance in overcoming it. If you prefer being surrounded by people like you, find ADHD support groups. These are composed of people who help one another conquer a common obstacle.

ADHD Treatments

You can get professional treatments for ADHD such as the following:

Psychotherapy

This kind of therapy deals with discovering and modifying thinking patterns to create desired behaviors.

Skill Building

You can receive training for developing practical skills that compensate for your weaknesses. The skills you need to build are particular to your own goals. This means you need to know what you want to do with your life. Once you know what you'd like to be doing, you can begin to seek help building your skills. Knowing the end goal is always a good thing before you start. It saves you time and energy.

Counseling

A counselor may help you come to terms with ADHD and find ways to live with it. Many local colleges and universities offer free counseling through their counseling programs. If you are struggling financially, you can certainly use this service.

Counseling is not the only option, but many find it helpful and productive. Like meditation or yoga, counseling can increase your ability to control your thought patterns. This can significantly boost your ability to manage your ADHD symptoms.

Anger Management for Men and Women

There are many serious reasons why individuals with ADHD battle to hold their resentment in line. One of the main reasons why outrage is a major issue in ADHD-affected people is the steadiness of emotional episodes. At one second, the individual is happy and bright; the next second, they feel disrupted and angry. That makes them act in an incautious way. One more reason for such eruptions is the pressure people with ADHD may feel.

Remember that you are not the only one attempting to manage your outrage. There are a lot of others like you who are also trying to keep their annoyance within proper limits. Thus, here are some useful ways you can deal with your anger.

Know What Makes You Angry

The initial step to defeating outrage is understanding what drives you crazy. Simply put, you need to recognize your triggers. Outrage can be set off by various circumstances, and these circumstances generally aren't the same for everyone. When you know that something is happening that might cause you to blow up, try taking some time off and quieting yourself down.

Make a note of anything that agitates you. Triggers can take on different forms and pose far more significant difficulties in ADHD patients due to their exceptionally low drive control. Some triggers are more intense than others.

If nothing else works, get in touch with someone you can rely on. Inform them that you will be calling ahead of time. Ask a trusted friend or family member if they can divert your attention away from the source of your annoyance. If you are unable to contact anyone at that moment, try counting from one to ten slowly and taking deep breaths.

Take Care of Yourself

When you take care of yourself, you give your body everything it needs to stay healthy. Your body can function properly only when it receives what it requires. Minor improvements in your health can decrease your side effects and assist in keeping your emotions in check.

Think about how this relates to anger management. Anger does not happen immediately. It frequently occurs because you have been holding things in for an extended period. You aren't dealing with yourself or seeing what you should be seeing on a regular basis. I recommend getting a good night's sleep when you feel overwhelmed by anger. A consistent sleeping schedule can boost your mood and increase your tolerance for annoyance. You must also consume the right foods, as maintaining a consistent eating routine is crucial.

Take Breaks

No matter how much you have planned for the day, you must take breaks in the middle of it. You'll quickly exhaust yourself if you don't relax and rest. Work is essential, but so is rest. If you're on the go for an extended period, you may expend all your energy and exhaust yourself. While you might need to work steadily, you also need to take breaks in the middle. That will give your brain time to re-invigorate and feel much improved. You want to allow your mind to refuel so that your explosions of resentment don't occur at the most inexcusable times. What might appear to be an insignificant complaint can continue to amass and become a genuine eruption of displeasure later.

Breaks should not be a now-and-again thing. You must incorporate them into your daily practice in a normal way, with the goal of remembering them. Take some time off after each hour of work. You may want to plan something particularly amazing for yourself once a month and a fantastic outing once a year. This will help you clean out your brain and return to work with more energy.

Think About the Consequences

This strategy has seemed to work for a lot of people. One of the most common things that you will notice in people with ADHD is that they cannot control their anger outbursts. In simpler terms, they do not have restraint. That is why you need to pause and then think about what your anger will bring you. Is it good? The most probable answer is no. So, take a moment to think: What if you acted in a better way? What if you changed your response so that it was positive? Also, talk to your coach or your friends about the incident that triggered your anger. This might lead to self-revelation. You never know what will help in your growth so that you can respond in a better way next time.

If you are indeed in an unbearable situation, you need to take a step back and think about the worst outcome. All things considered, the most noticeably awful outcome probably won't happen, yet you ought to be prepared with a plan in case it does.

Always Remain Positive

Remaining positive is essential to managing all issues in your day-to-day existence. You will undoubtedly encounter circumstances in your daily existence in which individuals press your buttons. How you choose to act in such situations is important. When confronted with disappointments,

ADHD patients usually end up going overboard. That is the reason why having a plan for each circumstance is important. Also, you need to have a Plan B on the off chance that Plan A doesn't work. This will ensure that you don't dwell on your disappointments and that you consistently have a way to move forward.

One of the most important aspects of being positive is to applaud and compliment yourself. Give yourself credit every time you suppress your anger and accept responsibility for the situation. You deserve it. This activity will boost your confidence significantly, and you will notice that your relationships with others improve.

Learn to Express Yourself in Other Ways

There are many ways to let out your outrage other than hollering, yelling, or causing a scene. Recognize that outrage is only a feeling; it is conveying the message that something is truly annoying you. When you do that, you will want to explain yourself better and, hence, put yourself out there without harming somebody. You want to be ready to have an appropriate discussion. To do this, figure out which words to use. The tendency to explode in annoyance is instilled in us early because anger is how we express our feelings when we are young. However, when we grow up, we have words to express ourselves, and yet we still turn to anger. Eliminate outrage as your method for dealing with stress and replace it with something that will not hurt others.

If you cannot talk to someone because of your anger, it is better to not talk to them at all at that moment. Reschedule your gathering and talk with them later when you are not angry. This will help you investigate their perspective without leaping to any conclusions.

To get a handle on your emotions, you may want to recognize and acknowledge the way you are trying to control your displeasure. If nothing works, talk to your primary care physician.

Emotional Regulation

Managing Emotions

Individuals are constantly exposed to stimulating situations that have the power to elicit an emotional reaction. These situations can be external (for example, receiving criticism or a compliment, seeing a newborn baby, or witnessing another person suffer) or internal (for example, thinking negatively or positively about yourself or thinking positively or negatively about your future).

The amount of attention a person devotes to a problem and the cognitive (mental) assessment of the circumstances greatly influences emotionality. Add to this the significance and importance they assign to the problem and their confidence in their ability to cope with the situation, which will determine their emotional response. On the other hand, the power, intensity, and duration of an individual's emotional response are determined by their emotional sensitivity and ability to self-regulate.

The Fight or Flight Reaction

An emotional response is defined as an individual's behavior and bodily expression of personal sentiments in response to a circumstance that they view to be relevant. The internal physiological changes that occur in an individual's body because of the fight-or-flight response being triggered influence the behavior displayed by the individual when they are triggered emotionally (facial expression, body movement, eye contact, and verbal expression, like the tone of voice, volume, language, etc.). The instinct of fight or flight is a natural protective mechanism. The physiological responses are many:

- The heart rate and blood pressure increase.

- The peripheral blood vessels contract to direct blood flow to the heart, lungs, and brain.

- To take in more light, the pupils dilate.

- Blood glucose levels rise because the heart, lungs, and brain need more energy.

- Adrenaline and glucose excite the muscles, causing them to tighten.

- The smooth muscle relaxes, allowing more oxygen into the lungs.

- There is a turn-down effect involving all non-essential functions (such as digestion and immunity).

When this reaction is triggered, the individual will also have difficulty focusing on activities and will lose the ability to engage in their executive functions (which further limits their power to regulate their thoughts, words, actions, and emotions). Again, this is due to the brain entering fight-or-flight mode.

Both real and imagined threats might elicit a fight-or-flight reaction. However, problems can arise when an individual's flight or fight response is activated too easily or frequently in response to a perceived but imagined danger.

Emotional Control

A person's emotional response might be either healthy or unhealthy because it can have a favorable or negative impact on goal achievement, social connections, health, and wellbeing. Emotions such as happiness, love, joy, and empathy, for example, can build, maintain, and strengthen interpersonal relationships with others. Conversely, experiencing and expressing socially unacceptable emotions such as wrath and aggression can disrupt or destroy interpersonal relationships and lead to social isolation.

ADHD and Emotional Dysregulation

Emotional dysregulation is defined as the inability to moderate one's emotional experience and expression, resulting in an overly emotional response. This overreaction is deemed inappropriate given the individual's developmental age and the social situation in which it occurs.

ADHD-related emotional dysregulation is hypothesized to be caused by poor executive function control. Due to a lack of self-control, the afflicted person might have very explosive emotional trigger sensitivity and emotional impulsivity. So, a high degree of impatience and low emotional impulsivity is characterized by a low level of tolerance, anger/reactive violence, and temper tantrums.

Such people have difficulty self-regulating their predominant emotional response. Individuals with ADHD may have such intense, overpowering primary emotional reactions that it is difficult for them to suppress the emotion and replace it with a secondary emotional response.

They have difficulty shifting their attention away from intense emotions. It can be challenging to lessen or modify a primary emotional response if you cannot focus on something other than the intense feelings. Problem refocusing can also add to thinking rumination.

Due to weak working memory, they have difficulty self-soothing to moderate their predominant emotional response (i.e., self-expression and visual imagery are impaired).

They display difficulties in organizing and carrying out an effective secondary response due to judging, openly manipulating, managing information, creating, and appraising various answers and their probable results, while also planning an appropriate response.

In short, people with ADHD are more prone to the following:

- Feeling and displaying emotions more powerfully, particularly during interpersonal encounters, which may be due to being overwhelmed by the feeling.

- Being extremely enthusiastic.

- Concentrating on the negative features of a task or event.

- Demonstrating irritation or fury by becoming verbally or physically hostile.

- Having social relationship issues such as social rejection, bullying, and isolation.

- Experiencing marital and relationship troubles, relationship breakups, and divorce.

- Having difficulty meeting work or academic goals/requirements, getting suspended or expelled from school, losing their job, or not being promoted.

- Becoming a victim of road rage and vehicle accidents.

- Having heightened psychological distress because of their emotional experiences.

- Becoming anxious and/or depressed.

- Having behavioral issues, getting involved in crime, and being institutionalized

Why Are You So Easily Irritated?

There are many triggers for irritation: getting cut off on the highway, your mother-in-law criticizing your parenting, your boss insisting that you work over the weekend, or your computer failing in the middle of a 40-page report that you have not saved. What do all these things have in common? It is the power to elicit wrath – pure, unadulterated fury, the kind in which you scream your head off and toss your phone against the wall. Not only are ADHD brains more susceptible to this powerful experience, but they are also more turned off by it when it gets in their way.

What Exactly Is Anger?

We all know what it is like to be angry, but do you know what's going on within your body when you're upset? Anger is the body's natural reaction to a threat. When we all had to be wary of lions, tigers, and bears in ancient times, our bodies acquired the acute ability to feel the danger. Thus arose a powerful mechanism to fight off the threat, i.e., our fight-or-flight reaction.

This fight-or-flight reaction is activated deep inside the brain to prepare our bodies (and brains) for a harmful scenario by either fighting as hard as possible or leaving as quickly as possible. We try everything we can to oppose (or flee) harm as hard and as fast as we can. This causes us to breathe quickly and shallowly (to increase the amount of oxygen in our muscles). It raises our heart rate (to get all that oxygen where it has to go) and even blocks access to our frontal lobes (so we do not worry about our to-do lists when we need to flee a charging tiger). What comes from all of this preparedness? It can mount slowly and steadily or turn on instantly with the flip of a switch.

What Is the Source of Your Rage?

Fury is only one manifestation of our bodies' "ready condition." So, why do we get that sensation in our bodies and feel worried, terrified, or even excited at times, and then feel like we want to strangle the person in front of us with our bare hands at other times?

Blame

Psychologists classify anger as a secondary emotion. That is, we feel it after we have felt something else. I know it does not always feel that way—sometimes it feels like there is nothing between you and your anger. However, if you replayed that single second of your life in slow motion, you would notice a flash of another emotion right before the rage. Maybe it is fear, frustration, or perhaps dread.

We have that uneasy feeling, and we despise it. As a result, our brain searches for someone or something to blame. When we locate the source of the problem, we may shift from the uncomfortable, agonizing, and ultimately helpless sensation of fear, irritation, or worry to the more energetic and action-oriented feeling of fury. What is the source of this sensitivity?

Recognizing Hypersensitivity and ADHD

It has been suggested that having a tag collection as a child is a guaranteed way to know if you have ADHD. Few things irritate an ADHD brain more than a nagging itch on the back of the neck, the tug of a too-tight waistband, the poke of an errant underwire, or the yelp of a nervous dog. All of the world's irritants function like sand in the mouth of an oyster, except that for ADHD brains, the irritation produces fury, frustration, distraction, and emotional overwhelm rather than a beautiful pearl.

Hypersensitivity is also known as hyper empathy syndrome, HSP, and sensory sensitivity, and it is common in ADHD patients. Hypersensitive people are easily overwhelmed by both physical and emotional stimulation. This can result in strong emotions such as fury and anger and in physical symptoms such as headaches and rashes.

Symptoms of ADHD Hypersensitivity

When hypersensitive arises, ADHD brains are more prone to be swamped with and irritated by:

- A loud and sudden noise

- Bright or flashing lights

- Quick-moving objects

- Strong smells

- Excessive information

- Coarse cloth or tags

- Too-tight clothing

- Hair rubbing against the skin

- The presence of too many people (can cause claustrophobia)

- Strong emotions (their own or others')

- Minor squabbles or frustrations

- Sensitivity to touch

What causes the ADHD brain to be extra sensitive? When you are contemplating something controversial, do you know that you should tell yourself, "Absolutely do not say that?" but then the words are out of your mouth before you have even finished that admonition? We frequently attribute this to a "lack of filter." It is easy to notice a lack of filter in the interruptions, abrupt outbursts, and odd jokes from the ADHD brain.

ADHD and Emotional Sensitivities

ADHD emotions are frequently more intense, abrupt, and overwhelming. These heightened emotions subsequently flood and overwhelm the ADHD brain, causing people to act rashly and irrationally. But when you look at what is going on, it all makes sense.

It becomes a system under attack. Because the ADHD brain lacks an information filter, it is constantly bombarded with information, sensations, and environmental stimuli. This assault puts the body's sympathetic nerve system, or fight-or-flight alarm system, on high alert, ready to assist us in fighting off an attack, fleeing as quickly as possible, or freezing in the hope that an aggressor passes us by. On the other hand, this form of preparation leaves us viewing the world as though it were ready to harm us. As a result, any comment, passing glance, or missed remark is more than likely interpreted as something intended to hurt rather than something unintentional or unrelated.

A Sponge of Emotions

Furthermore, because the ADHD brain does not filter information, it is more likely to pick up every passing expression and every minute feature of a person's face. As a result, emotionally sensitive ADHD brains are extremely perceptive and sponges of emotions. People with ADHD are often superb readers of other people's emotional states. They can feel other people's emotions without being told. While this can be a valuable tool, it is also agonizing. It means that you are required to feel your feelings while being vulnerable to the feelings of anyone else with whom you come into contact.

In an instant, you can go from zero to 60. The lack of a filter, which overwhelms the ADHD brain with sensations and other people's emotions, also makes it difficult to filter internal emotions. As a result, when an ADHD brain experiences a feeling, it experiences it at full force. ADHD brains do not regulate emotion (in the same way that they do not manage attention or action). They feel things either completely or not at all. It is not a dimmer switch but rather an on/off switch. So, there is no such thing as "just a bit irritated"; the system swings from "I am all right" to full wrath in a second. When you combine this with a system under threat, the emotional disorders associated with ADHD begin to make sense.

Physical Sensitivities with ADHD

Because the ADHD brain lacks a filter, it is unable to adapt to sensations. Rather than perceiving an itchy tag in an item of clothing for a split second and then dismissing it, the ADHD brain never stops recognizing the tag. Instead, it spends the entire day attempting to focus on the vital things, i.e., your professor's lecture, your wife's grocery list, and your boss's most recent request, but the tag keeps resurfacing. Thus, your attention has to ping-pong back and forth between the activity at hand and the itch at the back of your neck.

How to Treat Hypersensitivity in ADHD

Hypersensitivity does not have a specific treatment. However, because it is caused partly by the ADHD brain's problem with regulation, any treatments that assist with ADHD brain control are beneficial in reducing hypersensitivity.

Some examples:

- ADHD medicine (both stimulant and non-stimulant) is not hypersensitivity medication. However, ADHD medications help increase the brain's regulatory capacity, limiting how much it experiences something physically and emotionally. The drug also helps the brain focus where it needs to, tuning out what it must ignore the most.

- Exercise: Exercising is not just about losing weight and keeping your heart healthy. Many neurologists consider the positive side effects of exercise's primary purpose—supporting our brains at their best, which is especially true for ADHD brains. Physical activity does the same (and more!) for the brain as ADHD medicine does on a neurobiological level.

- Meditation: As a practice, meditation has been shown to have soothing and focused effects on the ADHD brain. This allows your system to return to a state of calm more quickly after it becomes overwhelmed. It also allows you to give yourself some space before acting from a dazed state.

- Nutrition: Keeping your body (and, thus, your brain) well-fed is critical for regulating emotions and feelings. Our brains consume 50 percent of our blood sugar, and without a regular supply, they cannot do the hard work of feeling just a tiny bit of a feeling or ignoring the car alarm down the street.

- Sleep: Getting seven to eight hours of quality sleep (not just before bed) nourishes your brain to its maximum natural capacity. Anything less than a full night's sleep begins to erode the body's ability to regulate.

Suggestions for Living Effectively With ADHD Hypersensitivity

Increasing your brain's ability to regulate will not heal hypersensitivity, but it will make hypersensitivity easier to manage. So, if you cannot alter your brain, adjusting your environment is critical to living a fulfilling life.

- Respect your brain: Recognize what works and what does not work for your brain. Do not make it do stuff that it is not good at.

- Give yourself space: If you become overwhelmed, take a break. Give yourself some distance from the things bothering you and center your thoughts. Then, after your system has calmed down, consider whether and how you want to re-engage.

- Block it out: Use noise-canceling headphones, blue light-blocking glasses, or other ways to block out all those extra stimuli.

- Set boundaries and expectations: Once you have identified what overwhelms your brain, you may set boundaries to safeguard it. Do you have a buddy who has three boisterous children and two barking dogs? I recommend meeting at a park. Have you been invited to a friend's lunch but feel overwhelmed in crowded places? Instead of having lunch in a large dining room, agree to share your lunch on a less crowded outdoor terrace.

- Share it: Telling others about your sensitivity will help them understand and respect your boundaries. Let them know how you feel (perhaps even share this book) and watch as views shift and compromises are found.

- Change things up: Feeling overwhelmed by the massive superstore? Instead, go to your neighborhood supermarket. Can't stand clothing tags? Commit to purchasing clothing with no tags. Do not subject your brain to the same number of stimuli over and over. Instead, start exploring ways to vary it.

Why Do You Become Enraged About Little Things?

Seventy percent of individuals with ADHD report having more frequent or strong rage than the general population. This makes sense at its core, as the ADHD brain struggles with regulation. It makes no distinction between which aspects of itself it struggles to manage. One of those things is anger. Rather than having a dimmer switch that enables only a small amount of fury, the ADHD brain turns its anger on/off switch and goes all in, being entirely flooded.

Overstimulation

Because the ADHD brain does not have a filter for irrelevant or extraneous information, it is under attack all day long, always absorbing an onslaught of extra stimuli. And while this is the norm for the ADHD brain, it still feels like what it is: a nonstop barrage. This activates our primary fight-or-flight mechanism, prompting the brain to seek out any potential threats. This notice not only keeps us (at least theoretically) safe but also has the added benefit of pulling us out of the uncomfortable state of anxiety/pain and into the more active (and, thus, less powerless, if not more comfortable) state of fury.

Irritable

People with ADHD who fall within this category are prone to rage. They are acutely aware of it on a regular and intense basis. They have difficulty getting over their anger, and they frequently dwell on the things that make them upset. In general, they experience more "negative" emotions (such as anger, impatience, frustration, despair, and hopelessness) than pleasant feelings (happiness, excitement, joy, etc.). As a result, they are prone to becoming trapped in negative cycles of aggravation, rage, and frustration.

The Influence of Behavior

However, changing your thoughts is not your only option. Behaviors are also effective. Do you have a negative self-image? Sure, your instinct is to get as far away from such feelings as possible. TV, the internet, social media, shopping, sex, and drink are all bright and dazzling numbing agents. They allow us to become absorbed in something for long enough that we get a brief respite. The trouble with them is that they usually do not give us much fuel, so we return to the original situation with less time and even fewer resources to cope.

On the other hand, fuel stops provide us with the space to gain clarity while simultaneously giving us the necessary resources to handle the issue. So, what can you do for yourself (or someone else) that will keep you going? Perhaps you can take a quick walk around the block, phone a friend, prepare a meal for a homeless shelter, pay a visit to your grandma, work on a creative project, or play with your kids on the floor. All of these things provide both perspectives and fuel.

The next time you are feeling down, remember this. Examine what your ideas and actions were doing. Were you on a downward spiral? Give yourself a mental embrace. Speak gently and sweetly to yourself, and then go over your list to see what you can DO to nourish yourself and your viewpoint. You can flip that spiral around at any time. Is it difficult? Yes. But you are capable of overcoming adversity.

Rejection-Sensitive Dysphoria (RSD)

Do you know how it feels like someone strapped you into an emotional rollercoaster without your consent? The idea that you can have everything lined up for a fantastic day—sleep, exercise, a solid plan—but one event can send your emotions into a tailspin and toss it all out the window? Do you ever wonder why you are so depressed?

If this is the case, you are not alone. You could be experiencing rejection-sensitive dysphoria (RSD), a condition that psychologists are still studying. However, there is growing consensus on what it is, who is most likely to have trouble with it, and what can be done to address it. So, let us get started:

Rejection-sensitive dysphoria (RSD) is a condition that causes feelings of rejection. It is characterized by excessive emotional sensitivity and suffering in response to perceived failure, rejection, projection of potential loss, or criticism. When faced with rejection, people with RSD experience intense agony, rage, or depression. The real kicker here is that it does not have to be an actual rejection. It could be the fear of rejection or even the mere possibility that they would be rejected. The same is true of failure: Sentiments of failure can arise even when someone does not believe that failure is a possibility.

What Causes RSD?

It is frequently easier to grasp RSD when it is sparked by true failure or rejection. For example, if someone with RSD performs poorly on a large project, they will not get promoted. This elicits a strong emotional response. It is excruciatingly uncomfortable, yet it makes perfect sense. However, the situation is not always straightforward because RSD can be triggered by potential, perceived, or even imagined failure or rejection.

Looking at a task list consisting of demanding projects, as well as having thoughts like 'I'll never be able to complete this' or 'I know I am not going to be able to do this, why do I even try?' can set off an RSD reaction. An accidental slight from a buddy can set it off, too. It can be caused by a fear of failure or even inadvertent criticism such as "Why don't you just set the alarm so you aren't constantly late?"

How Does Rejection-Sensitive Dysphoria Appear?

There is a spectrum of RSD reactions. They can range from minor melancholy, frustration, or discontent to full-fledged depressive episodes, complete with suicidal thoughts, excessive rage, hopelessness, or extreme social isolation. These feelings can be directed either against oneself or at someone else.

- RSD that is internalized: When a person internalizes his RSD reaction, it resembles depression. Internalized RSD is typically characterized by melancholy, hopelessness, self-blame, and self-hatred. "I am such a failure," "I never do anything right," or "I am so foolish" are common phrases. It appears to be sitting on the couch, hiding under the covers, procrastinating, or seeking distraction.

- RSD that has been externalized: Externalized RSD reactions are aimed against people or things other than yourself. They are typically characterized by sentiments of rage, severe exasperation, and resentment. Externalized RSD reactions might take the form of ranting, tantrums, violence or calm simmering, passive-aggressiveness, or even determined competitiveness. Externalized RSD reactions frequently feel explosive; it's as though they appear out of nowhere.

When a person with RSD also has ADHD, these feelings significantly influence productivity. For example, when you look at your task list, you might feel overwhelmed and distracted; you imagine that you will not be able to do everything. This produces the pain and agitation of RSD, which leads to additional avoidance and procrastination, which reinforces your idea that you cannot do it and worsens your sentiments. (For more detail on this negative spiral and how to break free, see The Shame Spiral page.)

How Can I Tell Whether I Have Rejection-Sensitive Dysphoria?

Because RSD can induce such intense emotions, it is occasionally misdiagnosed as bipolar disease, borderline personality disorder, or social anxiety disorder. The essential difference, though, is what causes the feelings. If the surfacing is provoked exclusively by failure, rejection, or criticism and is swiftly reversed by success, acceptance, or production, RSD is most likely to blame.

We are still learning about RSD; at this time it is not yet included in the Diagnostic and Statistical Manual (DSM-5).

What is the relationship between RSD and ADHD? We suspect that those with ADHD (and autism) are more likely to get RSD. We do not know why, but it appears to be related to ADHD patients' hypersensitive nervous systems. Of course, not everyone with ADHD has RSD, but if you have ADHD, you are more likely to battle rejection hypersensitivity.

There is some indication that drugs like Guanfacine (originally used to treat high blood pressure) can help with RSD symptoms. If you have severe rejection sensitivity, you should discuss a trial run with your psychiatrist. Medication for RSD is excellent because the symptoms can occur unexpectedly. On the other hand, medication may not help for every rejection, and it may not be a practical option for everyone. As a result, dealing with the thoughts associated with the feelings as they arise is an important next step that I strongly advocate. Here are some approaches for dealing with those thoughts when they arise:

- Recognize your patterns: Do you ever feel unwelcome at parties? Do you ever feel excluded in a group of three? Is an excessively extensive job list leaving you feeling overwhelmed and depressed in the face of certain failure? Do you get shaken up by constructive criticism? Make a list of the last five times that you were rejected or that your RSD was triggered. Does anything stand out? Knowing when you are prone to experiencing these feelings will help you overcome them more quickly.

- Thought charting: Writing down what happened, how you felt about it, what it triggered in you, and then the evidence for and against your interpretation, might help you bring your logical brain back into the equation and calm the rejection.

- The STOP method: Make some room, take a deep breath, observe, put things into perspective, and then go on. It is a tried-and-true CBT strategy for dealing with overwhelming emotions and not reacting with your feelings rather than your logical intellect.

- Exercise: A quick walk, a fast jog with music blasting, a kickboxing class, or another form of high-intensity cardio might help burn off the excess energy and aggressiveness caused by criticism or rejection. After you have burned it off, you might find it easier to talk yourself through the experience.

- Improve your self-talk: Talking to yourself as though you were a kind, sympathetic coach or a loving, wise grandmother can help you cope with rejection. Every successful self-talk session covers three topics:

Validation of Your Emotions

- Meditation: A meditation practice can help you become more aware of your thought processes, improve your capacity to let go of thoughts that are no longer useful to you, and strengthen your general connection to thoughts.

- Perspective-taking: Because RSD frequently reacts to imagined or perceived criticism or rejection, having a different point of view might be crucial in addressing the upset. You may ask a friend or spouse for their opinion or consider other perspectives that a caring and loving friend can provide to you. In any case, attempt to come up with at least three explanations for the situation and then choose the one that makes the most sense.

Impulsivity

In psychology, impulsivity (or impulsiveness) is the inclination to act on an impulse, with little or no forethought, analysis, or consideration of the consequences. Impulsive behaviors are often poorly planned, prematurely expressed, overly dangerous, or unsuited to the situation that frequently results in unpleasant results, risking long-term goals and success tactics. Thus, impulsivity can be thought of as a multifactorial construct.

However, a functional form of impulsivity has also been proposed that entails impulsive actions in inappropriate conditions resulting in beneficial outcomes. "When such activities have positive effects, they are viewed as marks of boldness, agility, spontaneity, daring, or unconventionality, rather than impulsivity." Thus, the concept of impulsivity comprises at least two independent components: first, behaving without sufficient forethought, which may be effective or not, and second, preferring short-term rewards over long-term ones.

In this chapter, we will talk about how to curb impulses and help your relationships if you have ADHD. We will discuss why people with ADHD tend to spend more money than others. They tend to not save up as much as a result.

Curbing Impulsive Spending

How can you decrease your chances of impulsive spending? That question may apply to any impulsive behavior that you have with ADHD. Of equal importance is how to cope with these issues in a relationship, given that the most significant things that couples fight over are sex, kids, and money. It takes open communication in a non-punitive, non-judgmental way. You can feel more confident about finances.

Say you have parents with ADHD who did not have a good handle on money. It could be a challenge to figure out how to handle your finances when the people you lived with growing up had a frustrating relationship with them. Both partners in a relationship have different family histories with money, which makes a difference in how you interact. Discovering the root cause of your spending habit is the first step. Second, you should modify the triggers and change your habits. Third, make a list of your spending over a certain period, then reread it and meditate. How can that help you financially?

You may identify with a few of the common ADHD financial issues. A higher rate of debt in the general population was found in a study by Russell Barkley. He discovered that people with ADHD have a higher rate of debt, particularly credit card debt, a higher rate of bankruptcies and foreclosures, and increased relationship difficulties due to money. If you have ADHD, you are more likely to get divorced; you are also more likely to remarry and get divorced again.

Sometimes impulsive spending can play into relationship issues such as the disorganization of financial papers. Say you are in the hospital and your family needs access to your financial documents; they do not know where you saved them on your computer or where the hard copies are stored. This can cause a lot of stress for family members.

The person with ADHD lacks investments and/or ways to save for the future. Most people wish to retire at a certain age and live off their earnings, but people with ADHD have difficulty seeing that far ahead. Also, people with ADHD tend to be underemployed, which means they are employed below their abilities. If you have a job in which you are not meeting expectations, you leave that job or are fired, and you start at the same level of position or grade. In essence, you tend to not rise through the ranks.

It is much more difficult for people with ADHD to get promoted. Hence, you may experience underemployment and struggles with making ends meet many times. It can be exceedingly difficult to save up for the future, and, of course, it is even more difficult to lose jobs and thrive with the pandemic. That's why, for an ADHD person, it is of the utmost importance to find a job that stimulates their interests and in which they can use their many positive capabilities.

Every time the ADHD person wants to be "normal", drama happens and the person enters a job cycle that is not made for them. It could be that the person exacerbated their weaknesses and never used their strengths. This situation happens to many people. We need to take a giant step to find jobs that fit our personalities. It's not optional; it's a necessity! Our happiness, and the happiness of the people around us, depends on this decision. A wrong job or a bad place of work or company will only worsen our lives and those of our loved ones.

A recent study shows that if you have ADHD, you have a shortened lifespan compared to other people because of stress and related health conditions. This can get worse if your financial needs aren't being met. Foreclosures can occur with chronic unemployment or underemployment at a lower pay than you deserve and require. Again, these are consequences of wrong decisions. We must figure out whether we are different or divergent, and we need to find our place in this world. It may sound simplistic, but I must stress this concept because I have seen many ADHD people fall into this trap.

You are unique; you need something special. Mindset is underrated, but it makes all the difference. Mindset means deciding to take control of our lives and not let anybody else decide for us. Mindset (the attitude we must adopt in our life to succeed) means setting a goal and going for it. I would rather fail to pursue my dream, looking for happiness, than feel miserable following other people's perspectives. People with ADHD tend to be people-pleasers to cover up who they are and blend in. They have a hard time accepting criticism and negotiating deals or salary increases. They don't have negotiation skills or even realize that they can ask for money without embarrassment.

Many self-esteem issues, as well as guilt and shame, get wrapped up with ADHD. But why do people have difficulties paying their bills? Such executive functions as budgeting and attending to bills are located mainly in the brain's frontal lobe. They include taking in information and deciding what is essential. These functions in the brain can be impaired by ADHD. You may have impairment in different areas of executive functioning. You may have a friend with ADHD, and their ADHD looks a little different from yours. Various symptoms show up, so planning what you need to work on will require you to adapt to the circumstances. What works for you doesn't always work for others.

Let's make it clear that no one with ADHD has the same shortcomings. I know people with ADHD who have brilliant business careers, leading to top jobs. Consider all the famous people with ADHD who lived extraordinary lives.

I'm writing a bit on the negative side because I'm hoping that you can discover the areas where you are weak, face them, and break the barrier. Knowledge is power. Knowing yourself is the best thing that can happen to an individual. However, we shouldn't focus too much on our weaknesses, as we don't want to forget all our beautiful strengths!

Let's say you have issues paying attention or, conversely, that your attention is so laser-focused that somebody could be calling your name and you would not answer because you are so into what you are doing. That is an issue with regulation and motivation, not attention.

You can learn from the consequences of your actions, but you forget the outcome and repeat the behavior because it was satisfying and fun. For example, the next time you have a bad day, you go shopping and feel better because you get a boost of dopamine and serotonin, which are low in the ADHD brain. Thus, shopping becomes a form of self-medication. So, you go ahead and shop again and your credit card bill goes up even more, which makes things difficult for the ADHD brain

When you are in a relationship, you might have a joint checking account. This can cause issues if you are spending money and not telling your partner. You may be doing what I call "sneaky spending": You are spending but hiding it. I also call this "financial infidelity" because you know that you are going to get in trouble if you tell your partner, "Hey, I just spent a thousand dollars on this dress." Instead, you let it slide, but the amounts can add up, and guilt and shame ensue. You avoid communication and the possible arguments waiting to erupt.

This is a gentle way to remind you to stop and think. Go shopping during off-hours. If you're in a crowded mall on the day after Thanksgiving and everybody is going crazy, you may jump in and follow the herd mentality, in which our brains tell us that we need to do what everybody else is doing. So, remember: shop during off-hours.

If you think excessive impulsivity is biologically programmed, go shopping when there are as few people as possible and when there is less sensory stimulation. Grocery stores are rough for people with ADHD because instead of three kinds of cereal, you have 500. You can stay in the cereal aisle or start talking to yourself out loud. If you are noticed, it becomes more than a little embarrassing. You are standing in front of all these cereals and do not know which one to pick. You would rather choose from three than 500. Before you go to the grocery store, you can order online or make a good ol' list!

A lot of grocery stores provide online services. They will put the groceries right in your cart; that is safer right now during the pandemic. Also, when you go to the grocery store, set a time and go during off-hours. You will be less stressed when there is a lot less sensory input. Stop and look at your cart before you check out. Ask yourself, "Do I really need this thing? Is this a need or a want? Was this on my grocery list, or is this just something I saw?"

Do you know the reason why candy and other unhealthy things are available at the checkout? It is about impulse buying. Read up on consumer psychology. It is fascinating how retailers use mind tricks to get you to spend money. So, you will want to look at your cart before checking out. "Do I need this stuff? Is this a frivolous purchase? Is this something I can't live without?" For example, you may need milk but you do not need a kitchen tool that you will use only once a year.

So, take that item out of your cart, give it to the cashier, and say, "Hey, I do not need this." Similarly, going to the spa, out for entertainment, or out to eat is a want and not a need; you can get food somewhere else, like your grocery store, and you don't have to pay extra for that service.

Therefore, you must take a look at what you are buying and distinguish want from need. I am not saying to eliminate the wants, as we do need to treat ourselves sometimes. However, we need to do it in moderation. Moderation is tricky with ADHD. We think that because a little bit of something is fun, a lot more of it will be even more fun. The consequence is that you end up having a higher credit card payment or facing issues with your partner.

Not using credit cards responsibly or not paying off your credit cards every month is like having a high-interest loan. You may have a credit card with a high-interest rate if you have a lower credit score. You can negotiate your interest rate by calling the credit card issuer. Some of the credit card companies have been pretty good about this and are easy to work with. Because of the pandemic, a lot of people have lost their jobs, so you can call the card issuer and tell them that you are in debt. They will likely work out a payment plan with you. However, be sure that this won't affect your credit.

Also, for online purchases, do not use a debit card. You cannot guarantee that someone is not going to hack in and take money out of your bank account. If you use a credit card, you have some protection against fraudulent purchases. If you use a debit card, that money is gone, and it is harder to get back. You can get a separate credit card, not connected to your bank account, for online purchases. Also, lower your credit limit; if you feel like you will go over your credit limit, drop the purchase.

You do not need math skills to create a budget. There are a lot of budgets available online. If you have a math learning disability, numbers can be daunting, but you do not have to do any math now that good budget apps are available. These apps do the work for you, so it is a dynamic budget, not static, which means that things can change from month to month.

Here are two apps for budgeting that you can check out: a paid one (https://www.youneedabudget.com/) and a free one (https://www.askzeta.com/) (no affiliate link).

You may need to spend more on dental visits one month if you need X-rays and do not have dental insurance. It is not necessary to visit the dentist the next month, but you should ensure that you have enough money in your "pot" so that you do not go overboard when you visit the dentist.

Divide your expenses by 12, then put a little bit in each pot every month. That way, you will experience a lot less stress, as money will be available when you need it for things like car repairs. Once you start building up your assets and decreasing your debts, your money will last longer. There is a way to determine your net worth: Basically, how much money do you have after expenses? It can be scary to figure out what you have if you are out of control and fail to budget.

Money tends to be one of the biggest things couples fight about in marriage, ADD or not. It is usually one of the issues they need to discuss, and they tend to have more emotions regarding it. Now, money does not have a preset emotional value. Instead, we attach value to it. Some of that has to do with our relationship with money.

Here is another common scenario: You are spending money on religious activities without proper checks and balances. If you have vastly different views about how much money you are going to give to your religious entity, or how often, you and your partner might face a disagreement. It may be something you can sit down and talk about at the kitchen table or with your counselor or religious leader. But, again, you know that, in the end, money is neither good nor bad. It is the value we ascribe to money that is at stake. So, if the household money is being used for something you both are not morally okay with, that is a top priority to resolve as a couple.

Whoever is more organized or has a background in finances might want to be put in charge of the money. However, the other person has equal financial rights. Sometimes, financial abuse occurs in relationships, when one person says, "Well, you have ADHD and cannot handle the money." Then, they take over tracking the money, and the other person cannot access it or even ask what is in the accounts. Instead, they are given an allowance. That constitutes financial abuse. As the ADHD person, you have the right to know what is going on with your money. If money is used as an incentive in the relationship and held as a reward or punishment, it is time to go to couple's therapy.

There is a type of therapy in which both a therapist and a financial professional or advisor are in the room. The therapist handles the therapy part, while the financial professional handles the money part. In one study, couples with ADHD found this to be very helpful. They could talk about their money issues with people who represented each part of the issue. This is a very good approach to therapy.

ADHD requires stimulant medication. After 30-40 years of studies, stimulant medication is still recognized as the most effective treatment for ADHD versus non-stimulant medication alone. It gives you some time to think before making an impulse buy. Sometimes just a few split seconds can help you make a better decision, one in your best interest. It also serves as a filter during money discussions, especially if your frustration level increases, and helps delay the instant gratification at the heart of overspending or any type of excess.

 If you are not treating your ADHD, you are more likely to pursue CBT or cognitive behavioral therapy, especially if you have guilt and shame about money. A therapist can assist you in resolving these issues, and CBT is quite effective in treating ADHD.

So, is there hope for getting healthy when it comes to financial issues? A lot of people are in crisis nowadays due to the pandemic, but please get your ADHD evaluated and seek good treatment. If you feel that your treatment is not working, talk to your prescriber or therapist and see if you can get on a better track with your medicine.

If you can afford to get an assistant, have somebody help you with day-to-day tasks. Maybe it is just helping with filing, scanning, or whatever you need to stay on track. Seek assistance from both mental health and financial professionals. Some financial professionals specialize in working with ADHD individuals and their impulsivity issues. But be incredibly careful because some corrupt companies or individuals will say that they can handle your debt, but they also charge you for it.

Create a support system with the help of the right professionals. I have seen some people with ADHD do very well in managing their money. Ultimately, I think it depends on whether you are willing to ask for help. Also, it depends on how much time you take to educate yourself about the ways and means of money. Remember that saving money puts into perspective how hard you work to earn something. That is a valuable lesson for anybody.

The Procrastinating and Overthinking Curse

Consideration deficiency hyperactivity issue (ADHD) can appear at different phases of life and in more ways than one. It occurs because of distinctions in the cerebrum, which influence significant working abilities like memory, attention, hastiness, fixation, etc. For many kids and grown-ups experiencing ADHD, keeping up with self-guideline and focusing are two of the industrious day-by-day challenges that they need to confront. In this way, one might say that a characteristic solution for ADHD would be some sort of consideration preparation that helps sharpen their discretion.

While the indications of ADHD can be mitigated by treatment and reflection, these are not by any means the only options. Studies indicate that another great method of working on your concentration and quieting your brain is careful reflection. Care or careful contemplation involves strict practices like Buddhism. It comprises fostering a more noteworthy consciousness of all that is going on around you each second by considering your real sensations, sentiments, and musings. It can likewise be used as an instrument to advance mental prosperity. As indicated by a study led by ADDitude magazine in 2017, one-third of grown-ups experiencing ADHD use careful contemplation, and a little less than half of them have given it high ratings.

Is Mindfulness Effective for ADHD?

Just like some activities can assist in fortifying a particular frail muscle in your body, certain activities can help with your cerebrum. Care helps improve your ability to control your consideration. It permits you to zero in on yourself and trains you to bring your meandering brain to the present moment when you get otherwise occupied.

Unlike different medicines for ADHD, care assists with fostering your internal abilities. It helps increase your capacity to foster various types of connections, prepare your consideration, and reinforce your capacity to self-notice. Subsequently, it teaches you how to focus on focusing, with the goal being that you don't respond indiscreetly and that you become mindful of your passionate state. Contemplation thickens the prefrontal cortex, the area of your mind that is involved in controlling your driving forces, arranging, and centering. It also expands the degree of dopamine in your mind; decreased dopamine levels are present in individuals with ADHD. Thus, reflection helps individuals experiencing ADHD.

If you view long spans of sitting in contemplation as extremely overpowering, here are a couple of ways to get started.

- Take a Class – You can sign up for a meditation class to harness the power of positive peer pressure. Following routines can be hard for people suffering from ADHD; therefore, they have trouble sitting down for a long time. There are a few communities that practice careful contemplation. Some places offer eight-week programs with weekly instructional courses of 2.5 hours each alongside at-home practice. For the most part, they start with situated reflections for five minutes at home, then work up to 15 to 20 minutes.

  Additionally, they allow you to choose between rehearsing longer or replacing situated reflection with careful strolling. As some people with ADHD tend to be better at learning visually, some centers also use visual aids such as a photo of a cloudy sky to describe the principal concepts. The clouds address every one of the sensations, sentiments, and musings that cruise by, and the blue sky portrays a sense of awareness.

  For example, you may find that when you are in the driver's seat, your consideration regularly goes to the errands you want to complete. When you become familiar with checking in with your psyche and body, you can utilize the care methods whenever you start to feel overpowered.

- Make It Your Own – Individuals with ADHD are encouraged to use mindfulness while performing their daily activities. You can even practice mindfulness on your own. Simply choose a comfortable place where no one will disturb you, then sit down and spend five minutes concentrating on the feelings of breathing in and breathing out. Concentrate on how you feel when your stomach rises and falls. Eventually, you will notice that your mind is wandering off to something else – your plans for the day or some noise you just heard. Label these thoughts as "thinking" and then return your attention to your breath.

- Practice Self-Compassion – People who have been suffering from the challenges of ADHD for several years can be left with crippled self-esteem. You can learn to accept your weaknesses and strengths through self-compassion. An attitude of acceptance can also help improve and manage your areas of weakness. For instance, if you are more compassionate toward your problems with time management, you don't have to pretend that you don't have a problem. You can get proactive about obtaining the instruments to oversee your time appropriately, which will prevent feelings of guilt over being late.

Studies looking at non-pharmacological intercessions for people experiencing ADHD have expanded as of late and suggested a few new treatment choices for patients. Current observational investigations back the rationale behind utilizing care methods to ease ADHD. In one review, a care reflection program directed in a gathering was managed to an example of teenagers and grown-ups with ADHD for quite a long time. Pre- and post-treatment evaluations showed an improvement in restless, burdensome, hyperactive-indiscreet, and preoccupied symptoms.

Another review, published in the Journal of Child and Family Studies in 2011, concentrated on the result of a care-based preparation program that was held for about two months (Saskia van der Oord, 2011). The participants included children from eight to 12 years. Careful preparation was likewise being led for their folks. The review revealed a critical lessening in the manifestations of ADHD, as accounted for by the guardians after the eight-week preparation program. There was likewise a decline in over-reactivity and parental stress.

Control/Ease Anxiety and Stress

Tasks like skating, whitewater rafting, mountain trekking, rock climbing, acrobatics, ice skating, expressive dance, and hand-to-hand fighting are awesome for grown-ups experiencing ADHD.

The particular stimuli that are used to perform this type of activity energize an enormous amount of brain areas that help control exceptional concentration and attention, restraint, error association, switching, outcome evaluation, sequencing, timing, and balance control.

Participating in these exercises also becomes a matter of endurance – preventing from harming yourself by loosing equilibrium, or from suffering a karate slash. Such activities also help you take advantage of the concentrating force of your brain's instinctive reaction.

Exercise likewise directs the amygdala and positively affects the limbic framework. The amygdala can help people with ADHD by dulling their trigger responses, which can be redirected more positively. This keeps you from getting carried away and creating a scene out of anger.

ANXIETY AND STRESS ARE THE WORST ENEMIES OF A RELATIONSHIP!

To make a difference in someone's life, you don't have to be brilliant, rich, beautiful, or perfect. You just have to care. –Mandy Hale

The Perfectionism Shame and the Frustration Wheel

Shame is something that lots of adult ADHD patients feel, and it can be deafening. The root cause of shame is primarily the fact that ADHD patients feel they have been unable to keep up with others' expectations and have been failures throughout their lives. If not addressed, this sense of failure can hamper self-esteem and become a huge emotional burden. So, it would be best if you never were afraid to go to someone and ask for

help, especially professional help. If you feel sorry and perpetually unworthy, you are a victim of ADHD shame. It can be a haunting thing to endure for a lifetime. That is why it is important to find the root cause of your shame, understand why you have to do something about it, and then take the necessary steps.

What Is Shame?

Though it might seem unrealistic, people misunderstand the shame concept and mix it up with other feelings. To prevent this, you must comprehensively understand what shame is. If you struggle with ADHD, you already know that every day it feels like you keep apologizing to others for something or the other. It might be because you didn't do the laundry, didn't clean your desk, were late to the office, or lost your car keys. No matter how hard ADHD patients try, these things keep happening over and over again.

This leads to a cycle of self-blame in which apologizing for even insignificant things becomes a habit. It happens even more in those patients who were diagnosed with ADHD later in life. Ultimately, these patients are numbed by a sense of shame, which can be very crippling. Things can get so bad that people refrain from looking into their wardrobe because they know it's messy, and they are ashamed of it. They feel tortured about every disorganized part of their lives.

Thus, when people experience shame, they are ashamed of a certain part of themselves. They struggle a lot in their daily lives, but they don't want others to know about it. They put up a façade in which they lead a happy life. But with time, this constant need to be someone else creates a feeling of loneliness that is exhausting. The patients start withdrawing from their close ones. Eventually, they can't ask for help from their family members because they are crippled by shame.

There are different types of shame in ADHD. We will discuss them below:

- The first type of shame is when the person is simply ashamed of the fact that they have ADHD. They cannot be comfortable with this medical condition. Though it is a lifelong condition that one must accept just as one would accept the fact that people have different hair colors, it is not easy to do so.

- The next type of shame that ADHD patients feel stems from the fact that they are different from others. When they look at others, and then they look at themselves, they notice significant differences. This shame of not being the same as others is more crippling in children than in adults. Everyone has the desire to fit in, but with ADHD, you will always have differences that make you stand out (and not in a good way). This constant attention that ADHD patients receive when they walk into a room gives them social anxiety. But it is not only behavioral differences that set them apart; ADHD patients often need extra help. They also have to take meds throughout the day and keep up with their doctors' appointments.

- The next type of shame that ADHD patients have involves their behaviors. They do not behave the same way as others. They almost always end up doing something that makes them feel embarrassed. For example, they might feel embarrassed because their work desk or their home is not as tidy and clean as others' are. Every person is affected differently when it comes to behavioral shame. But all of them have one thing in common: they are ashamed.

- Another common type of shame in ADHD adults is the fact that they are not satisfied with their position in life, and they feel that they did not put in enough effort. They had set goals that they feel like they didn't reach. The shame stemming from this feeling is worsened when they see others doing great things while they can't. This also causes resentment because ADHD adults are just as smart as others.

ADHD patients keep ruminating about their pasts, and they think about every instance in which they failed at doing something. It could be the time they missed paying a credit card bill or the time when they had to break up with someone special. It could also be the most embarrassing moment of their life. They replay the event repeatedly, and they relive that shame.

Note that shame and guilt are two very different things. You feel guilty about what you have done, but you feel ashamed of who you are as a person.

Consequences of Shame

Now that you have a clear idea of what shame is, let us move on to the consequences of ADHD shame. As you already know, people with ADHD face intense emotions. Whatever normal emotions they have are intensified to a great extent. Shame can lead to some pretty nasty emotions. Here are some of the common ways in which shame can affect the lives of ADHD patients:

- People try to conceal their personalities because they feel ashamed. They avoid any situation in which they have to be emotionally vulnerable. This greatly impacts their relationships. In the next chapter, we will explore, in greater detail, how ADHD impacts relationships. But for now, you should know that ADHD patients shy away from friendships or even intimacy because revealing their personality and who they are makes them feel vulnerable.

- ADHD shame prevents patients from expressing their emotions. They bottle up a lot of feelings. This leads to depression. The tendency to suppress one's emotions is more common in women than in men. They might be ashamed of an incident that happened to them, or they might be ashamed of the person they are. Whatever the reason is, the person keeps suppressing all their emotions and thoughts inside their heart. This eventually leads to severe mental health conditions.

- The direct result of both the above-mentioned consequences is that the ADHD patient is pushed into a state of constant anxiety, depression, and worthlessness. Their self-esteem takes a hit and becomes impaired. Every day of their life feels like a battle that they have to endure.

- Relapsing into more severe phases is more common in ADHD patients who face shame in a more intense manner. Someone who overcame substance abuse might relapse because they have a crippling sense of shame in the back of their head. In fact, there have been cases in which people purposefully gave in to problematic behavior just because they thought healing was impossible. This is why specialists say that, very often, ADHD patients don't consider therapy or any form of treatment because of their shame. They think they are worthless and, thus, there is no point in opting for treatment.

How to Silence the Haters

One of the main sources of ADHD shame is the haters in society who don't know anything about the disorder and yet treat it as an untouchable thing. The reason behind this is the several misconceptions that are present in society. If you want to deal with ADHD shame and not let it control you, you must silence the skeptics. We will talk about that in this section.

Very often, you will find that skeptics make it absolutely clear that adults cannot have ADHD and that they are simply using it as an excuse to cover up their faults. Skeptics keep saying that whatever symptoms they have or claim to have stemmed from the fact that their parents did not hold the reins when they were young. They will tell you to deal with your shortcomings and grow up. But I have already given you plenty of evidence in this book to support the fact that ADHD is real.

It is very real, and it happens in adults as well as children. So, if you do reply to the skeptics, do so with facts. A hard fact is one of the best forms of ammunition you can produce in front of the skeptics of society. You can even take a skeptic to one of your support group meetings or send them articles that will educate them.If you are looking for something sarcastic, you can always tell them how nice it is for them to be smarter than some of the world's most renowned psychologists and scientists.

The next type is the people closest to us but fail to understand that ADHD is a real problem. No matter how much evidence you provide, they will not believe you. They might keep telling you that there is nothing wrong with you and that you are simply being lazy. Experts believe that family members often behave in such a manner because they cannot accept that something like ADHD exists.

Moreover, they cannot accept that it might run in their family, so they go into denial. If you have someone like that in your family, you must stand up to them and let them know that ADHD is a condition that you are suffering from, and it is not about them. It might be difficult at first, but these types of people will give up as time passes.

How to Heal Shame

No matter how you reply to the haters of society, the shame lingers, and you have to figure out a way to heal yourself. Regardless of how qualified a person becomes in life, if they feel ashamed because of ADHD, no degree or educational qualification can reduce it. Not everyone can eliminate shame. There is some amount of shame in all of us but we can at least reduce the toxic levels of it. Here are some tips on how to do so:

- Educate yourself – The first step is to educate yourself about ADHD so that you don't have any misconceptions. Understand that all your behaviors and traits stem from genetic and neurobiological factors. It has nothing to do with your character, so there is nothing wrong with you. It is not your fault, and you have to understand that. Different areas of life are hampered because of ADHD, and you are not the only one dealing with this. Go back to the first two chapters of this book and remind yourself that ADHD is a biological condition.

  The more you educate yourself, the easier it will be for you to acknowledge that ADHD is, in fact, a neurological condition. You will realize that many of the causes of your shame are simply the results of your ADHD. With time, you will see how the majority of shame was self-inflicted.

- Have your own support system – If you don't have people supporting you in your journey to fight ADHD, you need to find some right now. Perhaps you can attend a local support group where you go to meet similar people and share your experiences. Or you could talk to a therapist or a family member who truly understands and supports you. When you connect with people who understand the problem, you will feel heard. If you have a busy lifestyle and think that you cannot make time for support groups in your locality, you can search for online support groups. Some of them even conduct webinars from time to time.

- Change your mindset – Pay attention to how you think and talk about yourself. Do you talk too much in the negative? Do you say things like "I am never going to become good at managing time"? If yes, then it is time you change these things. Instead, say "I know it is difficult, but I can slowly learn how to manage my time." Such a sentence promotes hope and motivation. Several people think that creating a shift in your mindset is about neglecting the problem. But that is not the case – you have to change yourself into a positive person who is open to all possibilities. You must let go of your limiting beliefs, stop judging yourself, and start believing that it is okay to make mistakes as long as you are ready to fix them.

Practice Self-Love

Loving yourself can be really helpful in overcoming ADHD shame. You may find it strange and difficult at first because you are used to blaming yourself for every small thing and being ashamed of who you are. Put yourself first and look out for your happiness and well-being. This will help you to heal from shame. Let us discuss some of the self-love practices that you can engage in to become a fully functioning and self-sufficient individual who takes care of themselves and lives a happy life.

Accept Help from Others

If you love yourself, never hesitate to ask for and receive help. Human beings are social creatures; we need each other to survive. When you are overwhelmed, anxious, confused, or lonely, make sure that you reach out to people instead of sinking into your own grief and shame. Sometimes good company can provide you with guidance and comfort. If you let your grief and emotions get the best of you, then you will not be able to calm yourself. People think that asking for help is what weak people do, but that is not the case. If you help others in their difficult times, then you deserve to get helped in your crisis as well. When your problems are serious and persistent, go to your friends, your family, or a professional practitioner like a therapist.

Meet Your Own Needs

Pay attention to yourself and cater to your needs. If you keep worrying about meeting the needs of others and neglect your own needs and concerns, you will end up nowhere. It is high time that you stop all these things and start putting yourself first. If are used to having someone else take care of all your needs, then you need to stop that as well. With ADHD, it can be difficult, but doing some things on your own will make you feel better. Make sure that you meet your basic physical needs like a dental checkups, medical checkups, exercise, rest, food, etc.

Pay a little extra attention to those needs and requirements that you are most likely to overlook. When you feel tired, confused, overwhelmed, afraid, angry, sad, lonely, or victimized, ask yourself what will comfort you. The reason for your depression may also be the fact that you have been neglecting yourself for a long time.

Start Having Fun

Start planning hobbies, recreational activities, etc. If you keep focusing on the gloomy side of life and constantly stay overwhelmed by your problems, your life will become a competition or a struggle for achievement and endurance. Life should not be a burden, so don't be too hard on yourself. Sometimes, a little bit of enjoyment and laughter is all you need to get back on track.

Protect Yourself

Protecting yourself from mental, emotional, and physical abuse is essential to self-love. If you love someone, that doesn't mean you have to accept mean and insulting behavior from them. If you think that you are being abused or violated, stop wasting your energy and time expecting to change that person. Take a stand for yourself and cut them out of your life. In the section "How to Silence the Haters," I have explained some of the ways you can stand up for yourself. However, if situations arise that are not mentioned, be creative and deal with the haters with a stern hand. Never blame yourself for the hate spewed upon you by others.

Be Gentle to Yourself

Treat yourself with compassion and gentleness. Make your inner voice kind and calm. Blaming yourself when you are in pain or facing any kind of crisis will not do any good. It will just make things harder. When you have ADHD, these feelings manifest themselves more intensely. You may be tempted to distract yourself in situations like these and ignore your feelings, but make sure that you don't do that.

Instead, try to be with yourself. You are the one who should be with yourself the most when you are experiencing fear, anger, hopelessness, sorrow, or anxiety. The innocent child inside yourself needs you the most. Try to comfort yourself with compassion, kindness, and tenderness, just the way you do for others. Listen to yourself and start forgiving yourself. Embrace yourself and build trust in yourself. Never give up on yourself.

Start Accepting Yourself

Loving and accepting yourself includes accepting your shortcomings, thoughts, feelings, and appearance. You must try not to feel the need to prove yourself to anybody. You deserve respect and love, regardless of your flaws. Others will seek opportunities to take advantage of your flaws and weaknesses. Stop seeking validation from others; instead, accept your flaws and weaknesses. You can prevent yourself from being violated by others and become a spontaneous and authentic person in the process.

Encourage Yourself

Treat yourself with enthusiasm and encouragement. Maintain a positivity coach inside you who always encourages you to do things you love. Do not wait for others to compliment you or show you appreciation. Give yourself credit for what you are good at instead of taking those things for granted. Encourage yourself to make even the slightest progress toward your dreams and aspirations.

Express Yourself

Don't keep your inner self hidden for too long. Start honoring yourself and communicate your needs, thoughts, opinions, and feelings. Remember that you have a right to have an opinion that is different from others. You are unique, and you can feel and state whatever you want without owing a justification to anybody. If you start stating your opinions fearlessly, you will start earning others' respect. Don't worry about the fact that you have ADHD. Does having diabetes mean that a person shouldn't voice their thoughts? No, right? The same goes for ADHD.

Start Engaging in a Spiritual Practice

Spend more time with yourself. Regardless of your belief in God, spiritual practice will help you to create a deep relationship with yourself. Reserving some quiet time for yourself is a great way to honor yourself. Religious beliefs are not necessarily required for spiritual practice. By engaging in such a practice, you can find a calm, centered place from which to access inner guidance to experience harmony with others and yourself. When you invest more time in listening to yourself and finding the truth, you get peace, clarity, and confidence.

Find Your Strengths and Weaknesses

If you have ADHD, you've probably heard more than enough about your flaws, difficulties, and problems. The good news? ADHD can be a tremendous benefit in your life. You just need to learn how to use it correctly!

Strengths

Many people would describe ADHD strengths as "superpowers" because they are additional skills that their neurotypical peers lack. People with ADHD have a unique view of the world that those who do not have ADHD cannot understand.

- People with ADHD often have "big feelings" that can be informative in many ways. They are intuitive and have a unique connection to their emotions.

- The ADHD brain seeks new and exciting activities. It notices and appreciates innovative thoughts, motions, visualizations, and ideas.

- To a person with ADHD, sitting and complying for long periods is far worse than the risk of failing. People with ADHD, on the other hand, are comfortable with the risk of failure.

- Many people with ADHD prefer hands-on, active tasks. This allows them to discover practical solutions to problems.

- People with ADHD are highly creative. They will create new, exciting material, such as paintings or written works. People with ADHD often have something valuable to add when it comes to problem-solving. The way neurodivergents use emotional intelligence allows them to find solutions that neurotypicals can't. For example, Albert Einstein had ADHD.

- Leadership is a well-known trait among many people with ADHD. This is due to their willingness to say things that others may not and their tendency to be direct and to the point. They are also excellent problem solvers (a good quality for any leader) and work well in groups.

- People with ADHD frequently have a lot of social influence and charisma. This is due to their excellent conversational skills. According to a study, people with ADHD have higher social intelligence, humor, and empathy levels.

- Innovation is common among people with ADHD. People with ADHD are typically nonconformists who can generate imaginative ideas because they think outside the constraints that others impose. In many professions, innovation is a sought-after trait.

- Many people with ADHD, according to research, become hyper-focused. This occurs when a person is so focused on a task that they don't notice what's happening around them. This is a significant advantage because a person with ADHD can work until a job is completed without losing concentration.

- People with ADHD typically have a lot of energy. They are always ready to act, and their personalities are often energetic, spontaneous, and passionate. If you have ADHD, you can channel your boundless energy toward success in sports, school, art, music, business, speaking, and work!

- Because of their ability to be hyper-focused, many people with ADHD are productive and will finish a task once they've started it. In contrast to what people see and what happens, hyper-focus can help one accomplish any kind of job. For ADHD people, interest is the key to working and succeeding on anything they start.

We focus on the problems far too often, which causes us to lose sight of the tremendous positive qualities we possess. This is especially true for people with ADHD, as we tend to underestimate our strengths and overestimate our weaknesses due to low self-esteem. We need to understand how ADHD affects us and the challenges we face. Only when we know the mechanics of this syndrome and the specifics that afflict us will we be able to take care of ourselves and thrive. To apply solutions, we must first gain knowledge. In the previous chapter, I sought to help you discover how ADHD may or may not have influenced your life. Because everyone is unique, not all of the flaws or potential scenarios apply to everyone. As a result, you must seek to discover your unique combination of traits and thereby find your way to a life full of fulfillment. Remember that ADHD distinguishes you; accept and embrace your divergent mind, stop surviving, and start thriving. You are awesome the way you are.

Weaknesses

People with ADHD face numerous challenges beyond being unable to sit still or pay attention. If left untreated, ADHD may lead to social isolation and other mental health problems.

- Their surroundings heavily influence those with ADHD. As a result, they are more focused on the present and not on the future. This makes it hard for them to manage their time and meet their deadlines.

- People with ADHD frequently struggle with time management, leading to procrastination. Those with ADHD may also have difficulty setting priorities and remembering all the steps involved in completing a task.

- Restlessness is common in people with ADHD, as evidenced by the fact that they have trouble sitting still or they fidget constantly. They may also experience agitation, racing thoughts, and boredom due to restlessness.

- People with ADHD can focus on engaging tasks, but they struggle to stay focused on and attend to basic tasks.

- People with ADHD frequently perceive their lives as being chaotic and out of control. As a result, keeping organized and on top of things can be difficult.

- People with ADHD struggle to meet deadlines when they don't find the task stimulating due to their inability to focus.

- People with ADHD notice that their thoughts do not stop. They don't move at a leisurely pace and rarely follow the same line of thinking. Conversations can be challenging for people with ADHD due to how their minds work. When speaking with someone, a person with ADHD may have thoughts unrelated to the current context or situation.

- People with ADHD have difficulty focusing on a single task for a long time. This means they have problems honing a particular talent or skill due to their lack of focus.

- The auditory focus of some people with ADHD is severely impaired, making them unable to concentrate during lessons or daily interactions. They sometimes struggle to recall a chat that happened just a few moments earlier.

- Because of their inability to filter information, oversharing is common among people with ADHD. Oversharing can mean telling someone something they don't want to hear or telling meaningless parts of a story.

- People with ADHD are frequently bored due to the speed with which their brain works.

- Interest cannot be held for a long time, so people with ADHD find it difficult to retain jobs. Focusing, recalling information, and keeping on top of minor details all add up to a challenging time at work and school.

- Many adults with ADHD struggle with emotion management, especially when it comes to anger or frustration.

Other Issues That Adults With ADHD Encounter

Criticism

If you have ADHD and notice that you are more sensitive to criticism, you may be suffering from rejection-sensitive dysphoria (RSD).A person with RSD may experience a negative feeling, such as rejection, as an outcome of an innocent comment or perceive a minor disagreement as being very serious. This overwhelming emotional sensation can sometimes be internalized, resulting in a low mood and withdrawal from the situation. RSD is not currently listed as an official symptom in the current version of the Diagnostic and Statistical Manual of Mental Disorders, 5th edition (DSM-5). However, it exists and is common in people with ADHD.

Stimming

ADHD stimming, also known as self-stimulatory behavior, occurs when a person suffering from ADHD repeats certain motions or noises. The purposes for stimming can differ from person to person and their surroundings. Generally, it serves to discharge a surplus of energy (hyperactivity) to maintain one's focus. Tapping fingers or tapping the foot is a classic move. Also, making subtle noises by moving small objects or using the vocal cords to produce a continuous noise are a few of the "techniques" that ADHD people use when stimming.

Stimming becomes problematic when it is extreme and interferes with daily functioning or causes self-harm or injury. Extreme stimming rarely occurs; more often, it is just a disturbing noise for people nearby. Stimming treatment may include teaching self-control techniques and changing the environment when it becomes a concern regarding the regular conduct of daily life

For Me, It Is Difficult...

You are not the only person who deals with the difficulties that accompany ADHD. Many adults with ADHD struggle with mundane tasks like putting lids back on things, finding their keys, putting clothes in the washer, or finding the motivation to practice self-care. People with ADHD frequently avoid doing simple tasks such as getting ready to leave in 30 minutes and following a to-do list. They might not even start the most basic tasks because they find it difficult to do so. Furthermore, many people with ADHD struggle with taking turns in conversation and find it challenging to stay on topic.

Find Your Enemies

You can be either your best friend or your worst enemy. You can either build yourself up or tear yourself down. You can either get through any difficulties you face or add them to your level of stress and overwhelm. It is your choice as to whether you will see your weaknesses as something that stops you from achieving your dreams or if you use them to your advantage. As an adult with ADHD, ask yourself: Are you your enemy? Or are you your own best friend?

Find Your Way in Life

As an adult with ADHD, you can use your abilities to limit yourself or to find your path in life. When searching for the right job, look for one in which you have a strong interest. A hands-on, creative, and high-intensity job will allow you to maximize your abilities.

It is also advised that you look for jobs that will allow you to take risks and are ultra-structured. Finally, go with your gut instinct. You know what is best for you so that you can make decisions about your life. Don't try to be the same as everyone else. You are unique, so embrace it and use it to benefit yourself and your life.

"Don't aspire to be someone else. Use your fantastic brain and excel at who you are." —Carmen Jacob

ADHD and Relationships

In this chapter, we are going to focus on how ADHD affects the different relationships in our lives. Certainly, ADHD can lead to resentment, frustration, and misunderstandings. You will even push away the people who are closest to you. But on the brighter side, there are different strategies that you can follow to mend these relationships and lead a happy life.

What Is the Impact of ADHD on Relationships?

The usual symptoms of impulsivity and hypersensitivity can wreak havoc in different areas of your life, particularly your personal relationships. The situation can be worse for those who have not yet been diagnosed with ADHD or who are not receiving proper treatment.

First, let us look at the impact that ADHD has on your life if you are the one suffering from ADHD.

As you may know, being distracted at all times is one of the most common symptoms of ADHD. When it comes to relationships, being distracted can cause a lot of problems. Your partner might think that you are neglecting them. Being distracted at all times might also lead you to avoid keeping important promises that you have made. Gradually, your partner will start feeling unwanted and unheard.

You might love your partner very much, but because of the symptoms of ADHD, if you don't show that love, your partner will start feeling like they have been left alone.

The next thing that I want to mention is being hyper-focused. This is a tendency noticed in ADHD patients. Sometimes they become so hyper-focused on something that they forget everything in their surroundings. It is, in a sense, the exact opposite of distractibility. Your loved one might start feeling left out or unimportant because you can't seem to drag yourself away from the thing on which you are hyper-focused.

Next, let's talk about forgetfulness and how it impacts relationships. I don't think I have to emphasize how partners might feel if you forget important dates or a dinner that you were supposed to attend after work. Your spouse might feel that you stranded them. You might forget your share of the responsibilities from time to time, like cleaning the house, paying the bills, etc. Eventually, your partner will feel like they cannot rely on you for even basic tasks, let alone anything important. In this way, resentment builds on both sides.

We all know that ADHD patients struggle with being organized. They might leave their tasks without finishing them or keep piles of stuff lying here and there. If you are in a relationship with a person who prefers that things be kept tidy and clean, this can be a problem. Your being disorganized is stressful not only for yourself but also for them. This is what causes constant nagging in relationships with an ADHD person.

If you are a person who is in a relationship with someone who has ADHD, you might constantly feel that you are unappreciated, ignored, and lonely. You will find that your partner does not keep any of their promises or does not remember things that you wanted them to remember. In fact, you might feel that the person you love so much doesn't care about the relationship.

Now that you have seen how both parties in a relationship are affected, you can understand how destructive it is. However, you can fix it and get out of this toxic cycle. Read on to find out how.

Tips for a Healthier Relationship

If you want a healthier relationship, here are some tips to follow:

Walk in Your Partner's Shoes

Understanding your partner is the first step to mending a broken relationship. You must place yourself in their position and try to understand their perspective. Also, keep in mind that it is extremely easy to misunderstand and misinterpret things. If you have ADHD and your partner doesn't, you must understand that there are a lot of differences between you and how you think. So, if you truly want to understand your partner, it's to ask them a question outright.

Learn About ADHD

To mend your relationship, you have to know everything there is to know about ADHD. You will understand its influence on you and your partner once you know about the symptoms and why they occur. If your partner doesn't have ADHD, but you are the one who has it, it is all the more important for your partner to learn about this disorder. That way, it will become easier for them to understand your actions.

Acknowledge That You Need to Work on Your Relationship

Often, relationships falter because the partners fail to notice – or, rather, don't want to acknowledge – that their relationship needs work. Constant criticism and nagging won't get you anywhere. If you cannot figure out a way forward, seek professional help from a couple's counselor who has experience dealing with ADHD patients.

Take Responsibility

It is essential to be responsible for your actions. This benefits not only a partner who has ADHD but also one who doesn't. You can only progress in your relationship when you own up to your actions. The symptoms of ADHD can cause a lot of problems, but it is not right to put all the blame on the disorder alone. The partner is also at fault. No matter what your symptoms are, it is in your hands as to how you choose to react to a particular situation. Your reaction will determine whether your partner feels loved or ignored.

Now, there are some things I would like to say to the non-ADHD partner because even you have certain responsibilities. You have to understand what your partner is going through. ADHD can make a person feel constantly guilty, ashamed, and stressed. They are overwhelmed by the simplest things in life.

So, if you see that your partner is experiencing strong emotions, ask them to take a time out. Then you can talk the situation through. Acknowledge the fact that it is not always your partner's fault. They are not always unreasonable. Sometimes it is their symptoms acting up. Care for your partner the way you want them to care for you. Finally, look for ways in which your partner's symptoms can be managed. Once that happens, your relationship will improve.

ADHD in the Workplace

In this chapter, we will cover the difficulties encountered by ADHD people in the workplace. However, we must clarify that many people have succeeded and achieved high professional positions in their fields. Some of my patients have had careers as top managers and found ways to perform brilliantly in their jobs. Nevertheless, most of us have encountered one or more of the obstacles described below in our professional lives. Never forget the excellent quality that we have. To find the proper job, we must express the strength we possess.

The wrong job choice can put us in real trouble, making us feel inadequate and causing us to strive to compensate for the constant problems caused by our flawed condition. This leads many people to a lack of self-esteem and, consequently, to a state of anxiety, stress, or depression. This condition will most certainly exacerbate the symptoms of ADHD that are associated with it. We know that work is a constant that will accompany us throughout the years. That is why choosing the right profession for our abilities is vital.

The symptoms of ADHD will cause occupational problems for adults, much as they do for school children. Some adults with ADHD are very successful at work. Others face many challenges, including poor communication skills, distractibility, procrastination, and complex project management difficulties. Working with a career counselor, psychologist, social worker, or other health care professional specializing in career therapy may help you in the workplace.

Distractibility

The biggest obstacle for adults with ADHD can be external stimulation (noise and movement in the immediate environment) and internal agitation (daydreams). The following strategies can assist with these issues:

- Suggest a private office or quiet space or take work home with you.

- Use earphones, classical music, or other "white noise" examples to block out office noises.

- Work in a space, such as a conference room, with few distractions.

- Send phone calls directly to voicemail and answer them regularly at a fixed time.

- Include suggestions in a notebook to prevent your present job from being interrupted.

- Keep a list of thoughts that come to you during meetings so that you can interact better.

- Carry out one mission at a time. Don't start a new task before you complete the current one.

Bad Memory

When you don't remember deadlines and other duties, your colleagues can be antagonistic, mainly when you're operating on a team. Try the following ideas to improve your memory:

- Use a mobile phone to record and take important notes during meetings.

- For complex tasks, write checklists.

- Use a newsletter board or device recall list for notifications and other memory triggers.

- Learn to use a day planner in which you log activities and events.

- Write notes and organize them on sticky pads.

Boring Blackouts

You get bored quickly at work, especially with detailed paperwork and repetitive tasks, because of your strong need for stimulation. Use the following tips to avoid boredom:

- Set a timer for the job.

- Divide longer tasks into shorter ones.

- Get rest, drink tea, stand up, and move around.

- Consider a career with bonus tasks and minimum routine activities.

Difficulties in Handling Time

For adults with ADHD, time management can be a huge issue. Below are several tips for improving time management skills:

- Use timeline charts to split large tasks into smaller ones, with step-by-step due dates.

- Reward yourself for meeting a due date.

- Use alarm-watching tools, buzzers, planners, or apps for time preparation.

- Arrange your computer to beep five minutes before every calendar meeting.

- Avoid over-scheduling the day by overestimating the duration of each job or meeting.

> **"The word disorder connotes negative and degrading imaging of describing people with ADHD, especially with so many entrepreneurs, CEOs, business moguls, and celebrities who have successfully defeated ADHD. It is what allowed them to achieve all they did."** –Emily Dickinson,
> Poet.ADDers

ADHD in the Family

When managing a youngster with ADHD, families should fight with conduct, instructive, and unsettling formative influences. This regularly requires additional time, more planning, and more assets. More strain in everyday life is frequently connected to these requests. Such difficulties can be related to the monetary cost of dealing with ADHD and its related mental disorders.

When a family encounters persistent pressure, the children, like grown-ups, face a greater danger of acquiring mental and physical health conditions. A conjugal clash in families with an ADHD young person or adult is typical. Therefore, families should seek to boost their mental and physical health to maintain a balance among members.

Siblings

According to a study, 10 out of 13 families reported that having a family member with ADHD negatively impacted them. This review also revealed that interruptions in daily life were the most common issue addressed by people with an ADHD sibling. These problematic practices included verbal and physical hostility, academic underachievement, hyperactivity, and learning issues.

People with an ADHD sibling have described situations as debilitating, tumultuous, and "centered around that one person." They have likewise indicated that they did not realize what was in store for them and what impact ADHD would have on their lives.

These people have also stated that they felt misled by the verbal animosity, actual viciousness, and other manipulative, controlling practices inflicted upon them. Likewise, there is a feeling of disturbance because of the assumption that they should become caretakers for their siblings with ADHD. Such caretaking included giving them medication, assisting with their schoolwork, and, surprisingly, interceding with their siblings' instructors. All of this is exhausting for a parent, and even more so for a child.

It's not all bad, though. A few family members in this research said that they were glad to be able to help take care of their siblings. Most of them expressed feeling overwhelmed when they felt that they were being deceived by their ADHD sibling or when they had to face the stress of their sibling getting injured or causing problems. This, in turn, expanded siblings' apprehensions and issues, particularly where the study hall and school setting were concerned.

These family members stated that they felt disregarded and neglected by their parents, as their needs were not regarded as being as important as those of their ADHD siblings. In addition, they said that they tried not to place extra pressure on their families. Some of them said that they felt disappointed because of how much their ADHD sibling "controlled" the family with their condition. Households with an ADHD youngster rate their families as lower in accomplishment and association and higher in questions than do non-ADHD households.

Because of their activities, siblings communicated uneasiness about the ADHD kid "destroying" family activities and social affairs, which diminished their expectations regarding family get-togethers and trips.

Likewise, other family members shared feelings of weakness and considered themselves to have been denied their parents' love and commitment. According to research, if nurturing instruction is remembered as a part of ADHD treatment, it is possible to reduce parental tension and strengthen family connections.

According to the scientific community, both sisters and brothers believe that they are negatively and severely affected by living with a sibling who has ADHD.

One of the most common problems pointed out by siblings is the disruption caused by an ADHD individual's behavior. Some examples of this disruption include:

- Verbal aggression
- Emotional immaturity
- Physical aggression
- Poor academic performance
- Social immaturity
- Family conflicts
- Problematic relationships with family members
- Poor peer relationships.

Many siblings of children with this disorder describe their family lives as exhausting and chaotic. Some of them say that their families always seem to focus on their affected brother or sister. Most of them are never sure what to expect, and almost all of them admit that they do not see an endpoint to this ADHD-related impact on their lives.

Research has found that siblings of a patient with this disorder can perceive the disruptive effects in three ways: caretaking, victimization, or feeling of loss or sorrow. Siblings can feel victimized due to verbal aggression, physical violence, controlling behavior, and constant manipulation coming from their ADHD sibling. Many have also felt like they are not being protected enough by their parents, who are viewed as excessively drained or too occupied to participate. Siblings of individuals with ADHD feel neglected when all the attention is focused on the problems caused by ADHD.

On the other hand, as in my family, if parents can raise their children with the appropriate knowledge, the situation can be different. Most ADHD children are very social and creative; when they are interested in something, such as a game or activity, they can be great companions to play with. They are usually lively people.

To conclude, the effects of this disorder are not limited to a single person but may spread to the entire household and affect the overall family life. Knowledge of ADHD will change this situation because when people understand the cause and solutions, their lives will change! When dealing with ADHD, we now have far more knowledge than we did 10 years ago. Anyone dealing with ADHD, including parents, teachers, and caregivers, should take advantage of the knowledge we now have. Applying all the solutions will have a significant impact on the lives of ADHD patients as well as their families, friends, and anyone else who has a relationship with them.

How ADHD Impacts Family Members

ADHD can interfere with your daily routine if it is not recognized and treated appropriately. Therefore, early diagnosis and treatments are important for a person with ADHD. If you look at how families with an ADHD-affected member are formed and function, you will notice that, usually, such individuals are quicker in taking up relationships. However, in most circumstances, these relationships are unstable.

Such instability may manifest in the form of unplanned pregnancies, earlier sexual intercourse, multiple marriages, and more frequent STD treatments. In addition, early parenthood is usually present in such relationships, due primarily to unreliable contraception.

Most youngsters and adults who have ADHD are likely to start a family without giving much thought to the prerequisites for building a favorable family environment. Research has also indicated that, in comparison to standard families, families with ADHD parents suffer from impaired marital and family functions. In such families, the rate of conflict is usually higher, and the cohesion is low.

Other reports suggest that spouses who have this disorder usually hold an opposing perspective about their marriage and family compared to their partners without it. It is interesting to note that the partners without ADHD do not feel the need to compensate for the disorganization caused by their unstable companions.

Parental Skills

Many ADHD parents are doing well, and their condition does not result in poor parenting skills. Qualities like creativity, intuition, and empathy can improve how they interact with their children. As a parent of three, I know about the challenges that families face. I always use creativity and empathy to connect with my children, and we still have a fantastic relationship today.

Many factors come into play when it comes to raising children. ADHD is not a disability if you know how to deal with it. My son has ADHD as well, while his sisters do not. My children got along well, and my son was always very protective of his sisters; in return, they adored him. We had some difficulties until he found his way in life. Parental support is essential for success. While ADHD may be difficult to manage at first, you will discover that the condition has unique characteristics that make your life more meaningful.

From my experience caring for ADHD people, I know that this is not always the case in families who have more members with ADHD. Let's look at other scenarios and how much responsibility an ADHD person can be when it comes to different family members. We must not lose sight of the fact that a thorough understanding of ADHD intricacies will go a long way in parenting. Knowledge is the key to changing how ADHD affects you, me, and our relationships with family members and friends. Knowledge is power!

Another way this disorder can affect adults is by diminishing their parental skills. Studies performed on parents with ADHD revealed that the symptoms included inadequate monitoring of their children, lax parenting, frequent arguments, and over-reactivity. Scientists also found that such parents were not bothered when it came to maintaining discipline and showed less effective problem-solving behaviors when facing problems related to child-rearing.

The relationships between parental practices and ADHD are also worth considering when it comes to controlling the comorbid psychiatric problems in parents or conduct disorders in the offspring. For example, scientists have declared that dysfunctional parenting in parents with this disorder might cause the parental strain of rearing children with problematic behavior. Additionally, other studies indicate a link between ADHD symptoms in mothers and dysfunctional parenting.

Parental symptoms frequently result in low parental self-esteem and external factors beyond their control. ADHD symptoms, for example, were associated with negative parenting self-efficacy expectations in primigravida women or women who were conceiving for the first time.

Paternal ADHD, on the other hand, may cause lower academic performance, even in children without this disorder. This decrease proves that the parents' impaired self-esteem and educational capabilities are not just a reaction to the increasing demands raised by their child without ADHD.

In most cases, parents with this disorder are aware that their parenting skills are insufficient. As a result, they sometimes express their feelings and emotions regarding this insufficiency. This expression, however, may cause further deterioration of their parental strategies.

Heritability

When it comes to heritability, parents are at a higher risk of having children with this problem. According to studies, about one-quarter of children with this disorder have at least one parent with ADHD. Similarly, nearly half of parents with a child who has ADHD have this disorder themselves.

While ADHD in parents is associated with ADHD in children, there are no differences between children with persistent versus remitted parents. Similarly, parental ADHD plays a significant role in developing this condition in their offspring. Instead, recent studies suggest that both psychosocial and genetic risk factors determine its presence.

Psychiatric Disorders

Children and teenagers who have this disorder can directly affect the mental health of their parents and caretakers. This occurs when ADHD is not recognized and parents are unsure how to deal with ADHD children. As I have previously stated, knowledge is the key to raising ADHD children. I wrote a book called "ADHD Parenting an Explosive Child" that explains how to deal with ADHD children in detail.

If you find yourself in this situation, I strongly advise you to obtain the knowledge and solutions described in this book. It will save you a lot of frustration, anger, and blame and provide solutions to most of the problems you are having with your beloved child. This trend among caretakers falls in line with the heritability and co-morbidity patterns in adults with ADHD.

Children with comorbid disruptive behavior disorders further increase the risk of parental psychiatric morbidity, proving that it is closely connected to low parental resources.

Parental Resources

Research has revealed that ADHD in childhood challenges parental resources and commonly involves frequent marital disagreements and parental stress. The parents of children with this disorder must cope with many challenging behaviors daily. Examples include low frustration tolerance, risk-taking behavior, temper issues, forgetfulness, poor academic performance, restlessness, disorganization, and low tolerance to frustration.

Also, parents of children with this disorder commonly suffer from high-stress levels and psychological strain due to their affected children's externalizing symptoms. In addition, experimental studies show that the externalizing behavior problems in children with this disorder lead to higher parental distress, higher risk of alcohol abuse, decreased self-competence scores, and issues like anxiety and depression.

Most studies investigating parents with ADHD offspring have found elevated marital conflicts and stress levels.

Disruptive behavior and ADHD symptoms commonly lead to impairment of family functions. Additional studies have revealed that the effects of hyperactivity on the family are more significant in men than they are in women.

In summary, the symptoms that parents experience and the existence of increased family conflicts might be the result of the stress involved in rearing a family member who struggles with externalizing problem behavior. Again, knowledge about ADHD is highly beneficial. Without knowledge, focusing only on emotions and daily problems can be extremely stressful and lead to more significant issues. If you know someone who is in this situation, encourage them to learn more; it's the best thing a parent of an ADHD child can do.

Fitness and Outdoor Sport

For most people, exercise is suggested as a strategy to help them deal with the symptoms of ADHD. A few studies have uncovered that ordinary exercise is perhaps the best treatment for adults with ADHD. Exercising stimulates serotonin and dopamine, two hormones that ADHD people need badly. It also increases self-esteem, confidence, and a general sense of well-being and accomplishment. Sports involving teamwork benefit social skills and learning to interact with people.

However, a lack of motivation might prevent someone from being consistent after starting any activity. ADHD people have an issue with motivation, consistency, and long-term practice. Beginning an activity can boost motivation, especially if results are seen. Motivation can be consistently boosted by setting new goals. We should not be too hard on ourselves or set goals out of reach. On the contrary, short-term, reachable goals are the way to go.

This is critical because constant activity helps us positively dispose of the excess energy in our bodies. Here are some activities that can help reduce the indications of ADHD:

Walking

This is one of the most straightforward aerobic exercises that you can do. What's great about walking is that it can be done by almost anyone of any age group. All you need is an excellent pair of shoes. The benefits of walking double if you walk outdoors. Walking helps tone your leg muscles and increases your heart rate. Children and adults who have ADHD can benefit from being outdoors, surrounded by greenery. Research conducted on people with ADHD revealed that even walking in the park for 20 minutes can help improve their concentration.

Dancing

Many people suffering from ADHD regard dance classes as a very appealing form of social exercise. The best kinds of dances involve fast-paced movements that allow you to release all your extra energy. Research conducted in Sweden with boys aged five to seven found that participating in dance classes helped them increase their concentration while doing their schoolwork and also helped them to calm down. Dancing is an excellent way for adults to socialize and move to music. It also has a lot of health benefits.

Swimming

Swimming is another aerobic exercise that can help tone your muscles and improve your heart rate. It might be hard for people who have ADHD to be a part of a sports team because they must spend a lot of time waiting for their turn to play. However, people affected by ADHD can get a big boost from being part of a swim team; they can perform individually while still being part of a team. An individual sport like swimming can be an excellent exercise for this reason.

Yoga

Yoga is extremely deliberate and slow, while people who have ADHD are very hyperactive. However, research has revealed that yoga can be a good form of exercise, even if you suffer from ADHD, because it helps you focus on yourself. It trains you to focus on your own body and your relaxation. It constrains you to the present moment and allows you to become grounded. Doing yoga would, thus, be able to assist you in figuring out how to think and concentrate better. Calming your mind and thoughts is a priority in yoga, and it can be highly beneficial for ADHD neurodivergent brains. It is helpful to focus to center one's mind.

Martial Arts

Different types of martial arts, like tai chi, aikido, taekwondo, karate, etc., require your full attention both mentally and physically. In addition, martial arts have fixed rules to be followed. This helps add more structure to your everyday life. Martial arts can help you feel both relaxed and focused, which can help alleviate symptoms of ADHD. One of the most helpful martial arts is tai chi, as it is a meditative practice. It can help boost your concentration skills and relieve your stress. Research has uncovered that rehearsing judo can assist a person by creating elevated levels of fearlessness and putting a spotlight on different exercises. You also gain abilities like fine motor skills, enhanced memory, timing, equilibrium, concentration, and focus. The discipline needed for martial arts is very beneficial for ADHD people of any age.

Strength Training

You can pursue aerobic exercises such as jogging, swimming, and walking if you are just starting to exercise, then add strength work later to add some variety. Try activities like weightlifting, pull-ups, pushups, squats, lunges, etc. Like prescriptions, training can assist in lightening the side effects of ADHD. Here are a few hints to keep you on track if you experience issues with your attention span:

The Morning Move

Exercise first thing in the morning if it fits your schedule. Working out in the morning can help you get the most benefits when it comes to boosting your mood. It can also help you set the right tone for the rest of the day.

Find a Partner

Exercising with a workout buddy can help you take a break and remain focused while you sweat.

Keep It Interesting

As I wrote earlier, motivation and resilience can be an obstacle. Periodically changing your routine or the kind of exercise you do is one way to keep your interest up.

Mix different types of exercises into your routine. Changing your activity every week or every day can help you stay out of a rut. Just like any prescription, the impacts of activity can keep you going. Consider your exercise as a form of treatment. Try to practice for 30 to 40 minutes once per day, for four to five days per week.

It's up to you when it comes to which activity you choose. Simply ensure that it is modestly active, so that your muscles feel tired, you sweat, you inhale more diligently and quickly, and your pulse goes up. If you don't know how extreme your routine should be, you must check with your Primary Care Physician (PCP). Your PCP may propose that you wear a gadget like a heart screen to guarantee that you are capitalizing on your exercise. One proven weekly routine is the following:

- Monday: Weightlifting or any resistance training.

- Tuesday: Aerobics, walking, or jogging.

- Wednesday: Resistance training.

- Thursday: Aerobics.

- Friday: Weightlifting.

- Saturday and Sunday: FREE!

This routine is just one of the many you can follow. If you take martial arts or yoga classes, you must follow the scheduled days.

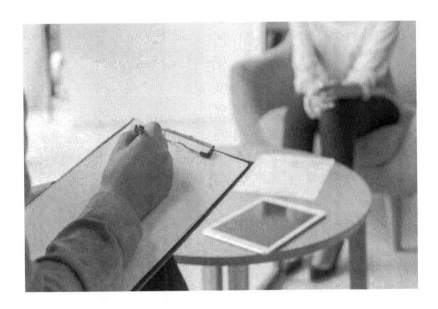

"The marvelous interplay of various brain circuits creates our instinctual reality of the daily life." - Abhijit Naskar, Love Sutra: The Neuroscientific Manual of Love

Alternative Therapies

Behavioral Therapy for ADHD

Medication can help an ADHD patient on a neurological level, but let's not forget the possible side effects. Also, medication does not heal ADHD; it just masks the symptoms. Instead, therapy is essential to making day-by-day life more manageable. Behavioral therapy is a critical or preliminary therapeutic approach that starts in the patient's childhood. In adulthood, the therapy changes into CBT or cognitive behavioral therapy. Before moving into the details of CBT, I would like to briefly discuss behavioral therapy in kids.

How Does Behavioral Therapy Work?

When we talk about going to therapy, we picture a therapist talking to their patient. However, not every type of therapy looks like that. In fact, behavioral therapy is quite different. Here, the emotions of the person are not the focus – the focus is on the actions and how they can be rectified.

When a kid or an adult is taken to a therapist, the therapist will first seek to understand the state of the problem and then prepare a plan to solve it. The main point is to eliminate all the toxic and negative habits and simultaneously replace them with positive ones. In the case of kids, behavioral therapy does involve not only them but also the parents.

This is because the parents are responsible for the child's upbringing – they significantly influence the child's mind. Many parents of ADHD kids get frustrated and start yelling, even when something is outside the child's control. So, a significant part of behavioral therapy is helping parents understand their children and changing their own behaviors toward them.

You must take a different approach when you notice that rewards are not helpful. That is when the concept of consequences, particularly negative consequences, enters the picture. If the patient does not do something as asked, they will lose points. This is what negative consequences look like.

CBT for Adults

Much research and clinical results support that adults with ADHD can benefit greatly from CBT or cognitive behavioral therapy. The patient shows higher levels of happiness, is more productive, and experiences increased self-esteem. Now I will tell you more about CBT and how it helps ADHD patients.

What Exactly Is CBT?

Is it any wonder that you experience extremely low self-esteem and chronically pessimistic feelings after a lifetime of errors, mishaps, and missed deadlines? Cognitive behavioral therapy (CBT) is a short-term, goal-oriented type of psychotherapy aimed at improving certain negative thought habits and changing the way you feel about yourself, your skills, and your future. Call this "ADHD Brain Learning." It is primarily a talking therapy, done over the short term to change how people think and instill healthy thought patterns.

Adults with ADHD have already experienced a lifetime of poor self-esteem, continually missed deadlines, and forgetfulness. This goal-oriented therapy, which involves mainly psychotherapy concepts, can help the patient change their thoughts about the world, themselves, and their future. All the negative thoughts are replaced by positive ones. In short, CBT can be regarded as specialized training for the brain.

Initially a mood disturbance therapy, CBT is based on the understanding that cognitions, or unconscious thinking, contribute to emotional issues. Spontaneous descriptions of events are unconscious thoughts. Such experiences, including mistaken assumptions about yourself (or others), a circumstance, or the future, are vulnerable to distortion. Negative internal dialogs prevent you from working toward a target, building successful new behaviors, or taking calculated risks.

CBT aims to shift unreasonable habits of thinking that discourage you from staying on track. It questions the validity of those cognitions, such as when you think, 'This has to be great or it'll be no good,' or 'I never do anything right.' Changing skewed perceptions and the subsequent shift in patterns of actions can help one manage anxiety and other emotional issues.

The Main Principles Behind CBT

It is believed that, in part, every psychological problem is somehow a result of unhelpful or faulty thought patterns.

Patients with psychological problems can learn better coping methods, which will help them manage their symptoms and lead better lives.

Quite simply, CBT is a goal-oriented treatment method that is very specific to the problem at hand. It addresses the behaviors and thoughts of the patient and all the challenges they are facing in the present day. CBT can be carried out in both group and one-on-one therapy sessions. It is a broad concept, and the treatment can be designed to focus on specific aspects of one's life. However, both the counselor and the patient must collaborate for CBT to work. There will be a series of sessions.

Initially, CBT was used mainly for people suffering from mood disorders. After that, it branched out to other problems. All of us have automatic thoughts as a reaction to different situations. These thoughts are the reason why we face so many problems with our emotional states. CBT addresses these thoughts and helps us correct our spontaneous interpretation of things. Our spontaneous interpretations are not always correct. The main reason for this is that they are biased and influenced by different types of distortions. These internal dialogs are so ingrained in our minds that they prevent us from making the right decision. So, your mental distortions hinder you whenever you are trying to calculate a risk or do something productive.

Once you start CBT, you will notice the significant impact it has on your life. Completing tasks and staying focused on a particular task for an extended period will become easier with CBT because the problematic thought patterns will have changed. CBT will challenge all your distorted cognitions, leading to a change in your behavioral patterns.

How Does CBT Help ADHD Adults?

Now, let's look at how CBT works to give you a better life. As you already know, ADHD significantly affects people's self-regulation skills. This, in turn, affects adults' executive functioning skills. It is also why ADHD adults suffer from emotional dysregulation, poor time management skills, inconsistent motivation, disorganization, procrastination, and impulsivity. However, all these problems are not yet included in the criteria for diagnosing ADHD. The criteria are still based on children. Thus, we need to change the way diagnoses are made for adults. Often, adults diagnosed with ADHD have a pessimistic attitude toward life. They are highly self-critical. The principal reason for this is that they endure several setbacks in everyday life and social settings. When situations don't go as planned (which is often the case), ADHD patients spiral into a cycle of self-blame. Even worse is that these patients start projecting their pessimistic thoughts onto their futures. They think that every coming day will be equally bad.

ADHD patients can't see the logic in things because their thought processes are clouded by their demoralizing beliefs and thoughts. This prevents them from growing and being productive.

Following are the distorted thought patterns that adults with ADHD experience. CBT helps in correcting all these patterns:

- Mind reading – This cognitive distortion occurs when a person automatically assumes that they know what the person in front of them is thinking. Such a distortion is very dangerous; people fail to notice what is right in front of them simply because they are too engrossed in their idea of things. They rely so much on their self-proclaimed ability to read minds that they sometimes end up misreading others' intentions. This leads to sudden bouts of frustration and anxiety. The direct result of mind reading is social anxiety. In the case of ADHD patients, this is even more magnified because ADHD adults already suffer from social anxiety to a certain extent.

- Overgeneralization – Overgeneralization is when people make broad assumptions about things even when their experience in that matter is limited. There are different ways in which overgeneralization can manifest itself. Mostly, it occurs when, once a person notices something negative, they start thinking that everything is going to be negative. In short, they allow one event to predict every outcome that is to follow. For example, if you don't get a job after an interview, you start thinking you will not get any jobs because you are not good enough. This thought process creates a feeling of hopelessness.

- Fortune-telling – This is another type of cognitive distortion seen in ADHD patients; they claim that they know the future and that it is going to be bad. The roots of this type of thought pattern are based on anxiety. However, there is a difference between making an educated guess and fortune-telling. When you are predicting things simply based on assumptions, you are fortune-telling as part of your cognitive distortion. Thus, the real odds are never considered, and so you cannot call fortune telling a real form of assessment. For example, if your job interview went bad, you can probably assess it, but there is no way of knowing whether you will get the job. There could be many reasons why you weren't hired. You don't know how your competitors performed or whether their personalities were better fits for the job. So, if you assume that you are not going to get the job even though you don't know all the factors, you are fortune-telling.

- Personalization is another type of cognitive distortion that ADHD adults experience. In this type of negative thought pattern, the person keeps blaming themselves for every bad thing that happened. Or the person blames someone else. No matter who the person is blaming, the situation was totally out of a single person's control; in reality, no one is at fault. For example, when

ADHD patients cannot perform well in a professional career, they blame themselves. They believe the results would have been different had they put in more effort. But that is not the case. ADHD is a problem with symptoms that will interfere with your daily life. You must find a way to manage these symptoms to live a better life.

- Comparative thinking – This type of thinking creates inferiority complexes and makes us feel that we cannot achieve things. Sometimes, the comparisons are not realistic, yet people continue to believe them. ADHD patients have been commonly found to give in to comparative thinking. Every person on earth has weaknesses and strengths, so you should not make comparisons.

- Mental filtering – This is a specific type of faulty thought pattern found not only in people with ADHD but also in others. When a person has the habit of mental filtering, they filter out all the good and positive things and focus only on negative stuff. In simpler terms, people who engage in mental filtering always regard their glass as being half empty. They are so focused on their dissatisfaction and inadequacies that they miss out on all the fun. Their feelings are often rooted in loneliness. The only way to overcome this condition is to focus on reframing your negative thoughts.

- Emotional reasoning – This is another cognitive distortion commonly seen in ADHD patients who think that their negative feelings reflect their reality. Let's say that you are tense and, consequently, that you think you are in danger; this is what emotional reasoning looks like. Often, it leads to exaggerations of insignificant problems.

When you engage in CBT, your therapist will help you understand your thoughts. Also, you will learn to identify the different types of cognitive distortions on your own. When you widen your perception of a situation, you can expand your reaction into something that is less defensive. With CBT, you will slowly but steadily address your fears and insecurities.

There are plenty of activities that the therapist can use to ease you into the process. You will receive homework in the form of role-playing activities and other assignments.

Over time, you will notice that you no longer jump to conclusions as you did before, or that you don't give in to a negative mindset as your default setting. One widespread problem among patients with ADHD is procrastination. Keeping track of time seems to be a significant issue, but not everyone suffers in the same way. The therapist will ask each patient to describe a recent situation in which procrastination got the better of them. The therapist will then set a goal for that patient. The goal can be something as commonplace as shopping for groceries.

The patient's relationship with the task is analyzed because this will help the therapist create a plan. After that, the task will be broken down into simple, actionable steps. Each step is analyzed to determine whether barriers might arise and, if so, what steps can be followed to overcome those barriers. While doing all of this, the therapist will ask the patient about what they are thinking during each step. They will also ask about what emotions are crossing the patient's mind and how the patient feels when they finally face the task they had been putting off for so long.

Another thing with which CBT can help is comorbid conditions. Hypersensitivity often leads to anxiety, and CBT helps address all the issues and comorbid conditions of ADHD. In the case of CBT, every situation is treated with a different approach.

How Does CBT Support People Suffering From ADHD?

ADHD is a chronic, recurrent delay in the ability to self-regulate, including executive functioning. Delays in executive functioning generate procrastination, disorganization, poor time management, emotional dysregulation, impulsiveness, and inconsistent motivation. Though these problems are not included in the official medical criteria for ADHD, they are associated with the disorder in adults, making it difficult for you to control your emotions and behaviors

As a person with ADHD, you tend to face more frequent and stressful setbacks in life's circumstances — at work, in social interactions, and in daily life. You are increasingly self-critical and pessimistic because of the number of setbacks that you face. This, in effect, can lead you to experience negative feelings, cognitive disturbances, and poor self-confidence. It is common for you to believe that you are at fault when things aren't working out. However, it isn't your fault. You can bring the same pessimism to the future, thinking that tomorrow will go as badly as today did.

CBT and Adult ADHD in Action

You may take medication to relieve the symptoms of ADHD. However, meds don't always work on their own. This is where cognitive behavior therapy (CBT) comes in. It is a type of talk therapy that can help with education, job, and relationship problems. CBT can help you feel better with or without medications and make everyday life easier.

CBT helps you understand how negative emotions create obstacles in your life. You are working toward substituting false convictions with true ones. A good attitude makes what you want and need to do easier. This starts a loop in which you feel happy, think more highly about yourself, and get more done.

How It Works

In the first few sessions, you and your therapist will explore what you want to focus on. Those are typically things that you deal with in your daily life. For example, you might want to learn how to make plans, manage your time, or complete projects.

You'll commit to an action plan to help you accomplish your goals. Programming time in between sessions for homework will help you learn your new skills in real life. For example, if you're always late, your therapist may request that you wear a watch and place a clock in every room in your home. This will almost certainly make you more time aware, but it's also important to find out whether your thoughts are playing a part.

You might think, 'I am always late; nobody expects me to be on time,' but this is not true; it's a thought pattern that you should change. Researchers claim that individuals with ADHD spend a great deal of time "putting out fires." CBT aims to adjust your thoughts and behaviors so that those "fires" never get started. It's important to remember that CBT is one of the best therapies available for anxiety and depression — conditions that are prevalent in adults with ADHD.

How Long It Takes

After 12 to 15 sessions (or around three to four months), you can expect to see improvement. You might find that you want to attend CBT sessions longer. When you spend more time in recovery, sticking to new habits is easier to achieve.

How to Find a Therapist

Most therapists use CBT, so you're not necessarily treating ADHD. Start by getting your insurance company's current list of available therapists. Then ask your doctors if they recommend anyone in particular on the list.

You may also want to:

- Call a local medical center or college psychology department and seek referrals.

- Consult the website Psychology Today. This site lists therapists state-by-state.

- Not be afraid to seek advice from friends and family.

- Ask questions after you have found a therapist.

CBT Vs. Meds

Many people feel that a combination of meds and CBT does the best job of managing ADHD symptoms. Maybe you don't want to take medication or do not like the side effects. In that case, CBT may operate on its own.

Speak to your doctor to find the best treatment plan for your individual needs.

Resources and Where to Find a Good ADHD Therapist

Once you have chosen to seek treatment, or your doctor has suggested it, your next step is to find an appropriate therapist.

Most people have zero clue about choosing a specialist or assessing a decent one. That's okay! In this chapter, we will look at the information useful in selecting an ADHD therapist for your child or yourself. There is no strict standard for choosing a therapist, as different counselors utilize different techniques depending on the patient. However, you can ask questions that will shed light on the sort of specialist to consider seeing.

What Questions to Ask When Deciding on a Therapist

The first few meetings with an ADHD therapist will be spent assessing the issues' extent and causes and the observed side effects. Because medications and treatments are generally interchangeable, advisors who gain practical experience in treating ADHD can usually deal with adults. You will be asked detailed questions about your interests and problems, including when and how frequently they occur. Be honest in your responses. As you progress, you and the therapist will reach a mutually acceptable goal regarding yourself, your condition, and how to best transform it. If you are dissatisfied with the advice you receive, seek the services of another specialist.

What Are Their Training And Qualifications?

You will want to make sure that the therapist is authorized to practice in your state. Specialists with solid credentials in ADHD, DBT (Dialectical behavior therapy), and CBT won't be offended if you ask questions about their qualifications, as they realize that this is an important part of establishing a beneficial relationship. If the answers given by the therapists are not satisfactory, or if they refuse to answer your questions, you should consult someone else.

Conclusion

At this point, I hope you have found reasons to improve your life. We are all different and ADHD affects us in different ways. Therefore, we must focus on those areas and start working toward a satisfying feeling. We are great as we are, but we can get better. Finding weak points and working on them one tiny step at a time will lead us to the desired changes. Working on our mental habits, expanding our self-imposed limits, investing time in our personal growth, boosting our self-esteem, and believing in ourselves is the way to go. I suggest re-reading the chapters that caught your attention for more profound meditation.

Return to your infancy and teenage years and then continue back to today to reinterpret your past life. Make it easy and enjoyable. Try to understand why things happened the way they did. Now you have the knowledge necessary to re-evaluate your past. This introspection will take you to a deeper understanding of yourself.

Think about what you would love to change in your life if you had a magic wand that allowed you to do so. Once you answer this question, you will know what to do and what your goal is. Thus, you can start moving in the right direction. Finding a purpose or goal is not as easy as it seems. You need a deep desire and a drive with value to make it happen.

ADHD people can change their lives; they need a vision, a purpose, and a strong desire. One of our strengths is that when we have a strong interest and passion for something, we can super-focus to achieve it. Let's use this quality to our advantage.

In this book, I wrote about problems, weaknesses, and difficulties you might encounter. I did this on purpose, to let you analyze yourself. But I must stress that you shouldn't look too much at your weaknesses; focus more on your strengths. Sometimes, we lose sight of the good things and focus mainly on the bad. Let's not do that.

Being grateful and positive goes a long way toward making us happy and satisfied. We want to turn ADHD from a curse into a gift. Use that gift to your advantage and find a way to live accordingly. In my experience as an ADHD therapist, I have seen many people make significant changes by following the above suggestions. I wish for you to realize your dreams the way you want. You deserve it!

I suggest reading a book by Tony J. Adams, called "Stop Overthinking," because I have found that overthinking is an ADHD-related obstacle that prevents realization. The author describes the root cause and the mental patterns that affect our way of living and how to overcome them.

The book does not directly talk about ADHD, but it touches on very important topics related to ADHD. Written with knowledge but in a simple way, it will benefit anyone who applies the solutions that Tony proposes.

STOP OVERTHINKING   by Tony J. Adams

ASIN:1803614609 on Amazon.com

DOWNLOAD YOUR GIFTS

Scan the QR CODE BELOW to download your free gifts. Thank you for choosing my book. These complimentary books will improve your life. Enjoy!

IMPORTANT

Your opinion matters to me! I would greatly appreciate it if you would take a minute to share your experience by leaving a review on Amazon.

Readers will benefit even more from your comment if you share a picture or a short video of the book.

Just scan the QR code below to go to the page for reviews. Thanks for your precious time!

L. William Ross-Child

References

Huaiqiang Sun*, Ying Chen*, Qiang Huang, Su Lui, Xiaoqi Huang, Yan Shi, Xin Xu, John A. Sweeney1, Qiyong Gong **Psycho radiologic Utility of MR Imaging for Diagnosis of Attention Deficit Hyperactivity Disorder: A Radiomics Analysis**

Kim, C-H., Waldman, I. D., Blakely, R. D., & Kim, K-S. (2008). **Functional gene variation in the human norepinephrine transporter: Association with attention-deficit/hyperactivity disorder**. Annual New York Academy of Science, 1129, 256-260.

Kooij SJJ, Bejerot S, Blackwell A, Caci H, Casas-Brugué M, Carpentier PJ, Edvinsson D, Fayyad J, Foeken K, Fitzgerald M, Gaillac V, Ginsberg Y, Henry C, Krause J, Lensing MB, Manor I, Niederhofer H, Nunes-Filipe C, Ohlmeier MD, Oswald P, Pallanti S, Pehlivanidid A, Ramos-Quiroga JA, Rastam M, Ryffel-Rawak D, Stes S, Asherson P (2010) **European consensus statement on diagnosis and treatment of adult ADHD: The European Network Adult ADHD**, BMC Psychiatry 2010,

Patrice Voss*†, Maryse E. Thomas†, J. Miguel Cisneros-Franco and Étienne de Villers-Sidani* **Dynamic Brains and the Changing Rules of Neuroplasticity: Implications for Learning and Recovery.** Front. Psychol., 04 October 2017. | https://doi.org/10.3389/fpsyg.2017.01657

https://www.imedpub.com/articles/managing-adult-adhd-comparing-nonpharmacological-treatments-and-

pharmacological-treatments-for-symptom-management--
amanda-lancelev.pdf

https://www.researchgate.net/publication/266682228_Bioma
rkers_in_the_Diagnosis_of_ADHD_-_Promising_Directions

Regional brain network organization distinguishes the combined and inattentive subtypes of Attention Deficit Hyperactivity Disorder. Saad JF, Griffiths KR, Kohn MR, Clarke S, Williams LM, Korgaonkar MS.Neuroimage Clin. 2017 May 22;15: 383-390. doi: 10.1016/j.nicl.2017.05.016. eCollection 2017

Ridler, C. First genetic risk loci for ADHD identified. Nat. Rev. Neurology 15, 4 (2019). https://doi.org/10.1038/s41582-018-0117-5

Zuss M (2012) The practice of theoretical curiosity. Springer, Brooklyn, Peterson C, Seligman MEP (2004) Character strengths and virtues: a handbook and classification. American Psychological Association and Oxford University Press, Washington, DC

Sedgwick, J.A., Merwood, A. & Asherson, P. The positive aspects of attention deficit hyperactivity disorder: a qualitative investigation of successful adults with ADHD. ADHD Attention Deficit Hyperactivity Disorder 11, 241–253 (2019)

https://www.ncbi.nlm.nih.gov/pmc/articles/PMC1525089/

The worldwide prevalence of ADHD: is it an American condition? STEPHEN V FARAONE,1,2,3 JOSEPH SERGEANT,4 CHRISTOPHER GILLBERG,5,6 and JOSEPH BIEDERMAN1,2,3

2 Slobodin, O., & Davidovitch, M. (2019). Gender Differences in Objective and Subjective Measures of ADHD Among Clinic-Referred Children. Frontiers in human neuroscience, 13, 441. https://doi.org/10.3389/fnhum.2019.00441

Radboud University Nijmegen Medical Centre. "Brain differences in ADHD." ScienceDaily. ScienceDaily, 16 February 2017.
<www.sciencedaily.com/releases/2017/02/170216105919.htm>.

White, H., & Shah, P. (2011). Creative style and achievement in adults with attention-deficit/hyperactivity disorder. Personality and Individual Differences, 50, 673-677

Forster, S., & Lavie, N. (2016) Etablishing the attention-distractibility trait. Psychological Science, 27, 203-212

Swartwood, M., Swartwood, J., & Farrell, J. (2003). Stimulant treatment of ADHD: Effects on creativity and flexibility of problem solving. Creativity Research Journal, 15, 417-419

Printed in Great Britain
by Amazon

16663098R00079